THE 50 GREATEST WARBIRDS OF WORLD WAR II

✤ LOCHLAINN SEABROOK WRITES IN THE FOLLOWING GENRES ✤

Adult	Matriarchy
Alternate History	Men
American Civil War	Metaphysics
American History	Military History
American Politics	Mysteries and Enigmas
American South	Mysticism
Ancient History	Natural Health
Anthropology	Natural History
Apocrypha	Onomastics
Aviation	Paleography
Biblical Exegesis	Paleontology
Biblical Hermeneutics	Paranormal
Biography	Patriarchy
Children	Philosophy
Christian Mysticism	Photography
Coffee Table	Pictorial
Comparative Mythology	Poetry
Comparative Religion	Politics
Cooking	Prehistory
Cryptozoology	Presidential History
Diet and Nutrition	Quiz
Education	Reference
Encyclopediology	Religion
Entertainment	Revolutionary Period
Ethnic Studies	Science
Etymology	Scripture
European History	Self-help
Evolutionary Biology	Social Sciences
Exposés	Spirituality
Family Histories	Spiritualism
Film	Sport Science
Genealogy	Technology
Ghost Stories	Thanatology
Gospels	Thealogy
Health and Fitness	Theology
Historical Fiction	UFOlogy
Historical Nonfiction	Vexillology
History	Victorian Period
Humanities	War
Humor	Western
Illustrations	Wildlife
Law of Attraction	Women
Lexicography	World History
Life After Death	Young Adult

Mr. Seabrook does not author books for fame and glory, but for the love of writing and sharing his knowledge.

Be curious, not judgmental.

THE 50 GREATEST WARBIRDS OF WORLD WAR II

A Visual Tribute to the Most Iconic Aircraft of the Second World War

LOCHLAINN SEABROOK
Bestselling Author, Award-winning Historian, Acclaimed Artist

Diligently Researched and Generously Illustrated by the Author for the Elucidation of the Reader

2025

Sea Raven Press, Park County, Wyoming, USA

THE 50 GREATEST WARBIRDS OF WORLD WAR II

Published by
Sea Raven Press, LLC, founded 1995
Park County, Wyoming, USA
SeaRavenPress.com

Copyright © all text, artwork, and illustrations Lochlainn Seabrook 2025 in accordance with U.S. and international copyright laws and regulations, as stated and protected under the Berne Union for the Protection of Literary and Artistic Property (Berne Convention), and the Universal Copyright Convention (the UCC). All rights reserved under the Pan-American and International Copyright Conventions.

PRINTING HISTORY
1st SRP paperback edition, 1st printing, August 2025 • ISBN: 978-1-955351-64-5
1st SRP hardcover edition, 1st printing, August 2025 • ISBN: 978-1-955351-65-2

ISBN: 978-1-955351-64-5 (paperback)
Library of Congress Control Number: 2025944748

This work is the copyrighted intellectual property of Lochlainn Seabrook and has been registered with the Copyright Office at the Library of Congress in Washington, D.C., USA. No part of this work (including text, covers, drawings, photos, illustrations, maps, images, diagrams, etc.), in whole or in part, may be used, reproduced, stored in a retrieval system, or transmitted, in any form or by any means now known or hereafter invented, without written permission from the publisher. The sale, duplication, hire, lending, copying, digitalization, or reproduction of this material, in any manner or form whatsoever, is also prohibited, and is a violation of federal, civil, and digital copyright law, which provides severe civil and criminal penalties for any violations.

The 50 Greatest Warbirds of World War II: A Visual Tribute to the Most Iconic Aircraft of the Second World War, by Lochlainn Seabrook. Includes an introduction, illustrations, index, endnotes, appendices, and bibliography.

ARTWORK
Front and back cover design and art, book design, layout, font selection, and interior art by Lochlainn Seabrook
All images, pictures, photos, illustrations, image captions, graphic design, and graphic art copyright © Lochlainn Seabrook
All images created and/or selected, placed, manipulated, cleaned, colored, and tinted by Lochlainn Seabrook
Cover image: "The U.S. Army Air Forces P-51D Mustang at Work," Lochlainn Seabrook
Title page image: "The U.S. Navy F4U Corsair at Work," Lochlainn Seabrook
Half title page image: "The U.S. Navy SBD Dauntless," Lochlainn Seabrook
All rights reserved.

All persons who approve of the authority and principles of Colonel Lochlainn Seabrook's literary work, and realize its benefits as a means of reeducating the world about facts left out of mainstream books, are hereby requested to avidly recommend his titles to others and to vigorously cooperate in extending their reach, scope, and influence around the globe.

The views documented in this book concerning World War II aircraft are those of the publisher.

WRITTEN, DESIGNED, PUBLISHED, PRINTED, & MANUFACTURED IN THE UNITED STATES OF AMERICA

DEDICATION

To the World War II aircraft designers, engineers, draftsmen, and test pilots whose vision and genius lifted nations into the skies; and more importantly to the courageous male and female pilots, crewmen, and ground personnel who flew and serviced these aircraft.

EPIGRAPH

"The engine is the heart of an airplane, but the pilot is its soul."

Attributed to Walter Alexander Raleigh, RAF Air Marshal

CONTENTS

P-51D Mustang. Copyright © Lochlainn Seabrook.

Notes to the Reader ★ page 13
A Brief History of the Two Opposing War Powers During World War II ★ page 15
World War II Aircraft Designation Codes ★ page 17
Introduction ★ page 19

SECTION ONE: UNITED STATES AIRCRAFT

1. P-51D Mustang ★ page 23
2. B-17 Flying Fortress ★ page 27
3. F4U Corsair ★ page 31
4. P-38 Lightning ★ page 35
5. B-29 Superfortress ★ page 39
6. P-47 Thunderbolt ★ page 43
7. SBD Dauntless ★ page 47
8. B-25 Mitchell ★ page 51
9. C-47 Skytrain (Dakota) ★ page 55
10. F6F Hellcat ★ page 59
11. A-20 Havoc ★ page 63
12. PBY Catalina ★ page 67
13. TBF Avenger ★ page 71
14. B-24 Liberator ★ page 75
15. F2A Buffalo ★ page 79
16. P-39 Airacobra ★ page 83
17. P-40 Warhawk ★ page 87
18. F4F Wildcat ★ page 91

SECTION TWO: UNITED KINGDOM AIRCRAFT
19. Supermarine Spitfire ★ page 97
20. Avro Lancaster ★ page 101
21. Hawker Hurricane ★ page 105
22. De Havilland Mosquito ★ page 109
23. Fairey Swordfish ★ page 113
24. Gloster Gladiator ★ page 117
25. Bristol Beaufighter ★ page 121
26. Short Sunderland ★ page 125

SECTION THREE: GERMAN AIRCRAFT
27. Messerschmitt Bf 109 ★ page 131
28. Focke-Wulf Fw 190 ★ page 135
29. Messerschmitt Me 262 ★ page 139
30. Junkers Ju 87 Stuka ★ page 143
31. Heinkel He 111 ★ page 147
32. Dornier Do 17 ★ page 151
33. Arado Ar 234 ★ page 155
34. Messerschmitt Bf 110 ★ page 159
35. Fieseler Fi 156 Storch ★ page 163
36. Junkers Ju 88 ★ page 167

SECTION FOUR: JAPANESE AIRCRAFT
37. Mitsubishi A6M Zero ★ page 173
38. Nakajima Ki-43 "Oscar" ★ page 177
39. Kawanishi H8K "Emily" ★ page 181
40. Yokosuka D4Y "Judy" ★ page 185
41. Mitsubishi G4M "Betty" ★ page 189
42. Nakajima B5N "Kate" ★ page 193

SECTION FIVE: SOVIET AIRCRAFT
43. Ilyushin Il-2 Sturmovik ★ page 199
44. Yakovlev Yak-3 ★ page 203
45. Lavochkin La-5 ★ page 207
46. Tupolev Tu-2 ★ page 211
47. Mikoyan-Gurevich MiG-3 ★ page 215
48. Petlyakov Pe-2 ★ page 219

SECTION SIX: ITALIAN AIRCRAFT
49. Macchi C.202 Folgore ★ page 225
50. Savoia-Marchetti SM.79 Sparviero ★ page 229

Bibliography ★ page 233
Meet the Author-Historian-Artist ★ page 241
Praise for the Author ★ page 243
Learn More ★ page 249

The Hawker Hurricane. Copyright © Lochlainn Seabrook.

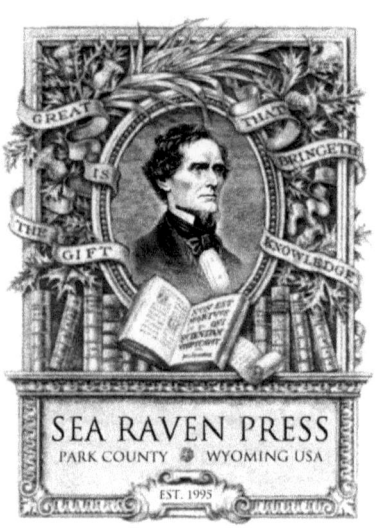

"Books invite all; they constrain none."
Hartley Burr Alexander (1873-1939)

NOTES TO THE READER

"NOTHING IN THE PAST IS DEAD TO THE MAN WHO WOULD
LEARN HOW THE PRESENT CAME TO BE WHAT IT IS."

WILLIAM STUBBS, VICTORIAN ENGLISH HISTORIAN

SYMBOLS, INSIGNIA, & NOSE ART
☛ While due to shifting cultural changes some World War II symbols are now considered offensive or inappropriate, this is a history book, one composed by an author-historian-artist who eschews presentism. As such I have retained as much of the authentic military art and symbolism from the 1930s and 1940s as possible. When dealing with history it should first always be read and understood within its own individual historical context; not as distinct propaganda meant to influence or disparage—as mainstream media and many modern universities maliciously use and incorrectly depict it today. Presentism is almost always the unhistorical and unfair portrayal of history by the dishonest and mendacious for political and financial gain.

DISCLAIMER
☛ I obtained the information in this book from sources deemed reliable and authoritative. Despite this, I cannot guarantee complete and total accuracy pertaining to every detail—especially regarding my illustrations. This is especially relevant considering the facts that: 1) there were hundreds of variations created of the aircraft listed in this book besides those shown; 2) that several of my planes are nearly 100 years old as of this writing; and 3) that even the most reputable aviation experts make mistakes. Thus I advise those with an interest in a specific aircraft to perform their own independent research. L.S.

P-40 Warhawk. Copyright © Lochlainn Seabrook.

British Prime Minister Winston Churchill, May 21, 1945, Paris, France. Copyright © Lochlainn Seabrook.

A BRIEF HISTORY
OF THE TWO OPPOSING WAR POWERS DURING WORLD WAR II
by Lochlainn Seabrook

WORLD WAR II WAS FOUGHT between two major sides: the Allied Powers and the Axis Powers. This history-altering conflict began on September 1, 1939, when Germany invaded Poland. Two days later, on September 3, 1939, Britain and France declared war on Germany, marking the official start of the Second World War. Let us now look at the two sides in more detail.

THE ALLIED POWERS
These were the countries that banded together to stop the Axis from taking over other nations. Essentially democratic in their values (many with classically republican leaders), their goal was to protect individual and national freedoms as well as put a stop to international aggression.

The primary Allied Countries were:
United States
Great Britain
Soviet Union (Russia)
China
France (Free French Forces after 1940)

Other Allied nations included:
Australia
Belgium
Brazil
Canada
Czechoslovakia
Greece
India
Netherlands
New Zealand
Norway
Poland
South Africa
Yugoslavia
(there were others as well)

Copyright © Lochlainn Seabrook.

These countries referred to themselves as "Allies" because they viewed each other as friends all working together against a common enemy.

THE AXIS POWERS
Now let us turn to the Axis Powers. These countries formed an alliance to expand their power and territory. Essentially autocratic and ruled by dictators (or at least powerful authoritarians), they believed in strong control by their governments and leaders.

The Main Axis countries were:
Germany (led by Adolf Hitler)
Italy (led by Benito Mussolini, until 1943)
Japan (led by Emperor Hirohito and various military leaders)

Other Axis supporters included:
Bulgaria
Finland (co-belligerent with Germany against the USSR, not officially Axis)
Hungary
Romania
(there were also a few other smaller nations)

ORIGIN OF THE GROUPS' NAMES
As noted, the Allies were united in a common cause to fight back against invasion, dictatorship, and oppression. The Axis powers were named for the "axis" (line) of alliance between Germany and Italy, which later included Japan. (The name "Axis" was coined by Italy's leader, Benito Mussolini, who intended that the world would turn around the "Rome–Berlin Axis"—meaning Italy and Germany would be the center of world power.)

CONCLUSION OF THE WAR
As we all well know today the Allied Powers won World War II. But this victory did not come easy. It was only after six long brutal years of fighting that they were able to defeat the Axis Powers in 1945. Estimates of the death toll range up to as high as 85 million people—3 percent of the world's population at the time. The cost of our freedom today, which we continue to enjoy, was paid for in human blood.

KEY REASONS THE ALLIES WON
- The Allies had more countries and thus more people on their side, with more soldiers fighting together as one great team.
- The Allies had greater supplies of food, fuel, weapons, and factories—supplied mainly by the United States.
- American factories produced massive amounts of tanks, planes, ships, and supplies, helping the Allies win battles all over the world.
- The Allied countries worked together to plan strategies and share information.
- Axis leaders made numerous poor decisions—such as attacking too many countries simultaneously. Germany even invaded the Soviet Union, a costly mistake for the Axis.
- Turning Points included major battles, such as the Battle of Stalingrad, D-Day, and the Battle of Midway, all which helped shift the war in favor of the Allies.

On May 8, 1945, Germany surrendered to the Allies in Europe. In August 1945 Japan conceded after atomic bombs were dropped on Hiroshima (Aug. 6) and Nagasaki (Aug. 9), formerly surrendering on September 2, 1945, aboard the USS *Missouri*. Hence World War II came to an end with the Allies victorious.

WWII AIRCRAFT DESIGNATION CODES

by Lochlainn Seabrook

CODE	MEANING	USED BY
F (role code)	"Fighter"	Navy
B (role code)	"Bomber"	Navy
SB (role code)	"Scout Bomber"	Navy
TB (role code)	"Torpedo Bomber"	Navy
P (role code)	"Patrol"	Navy
J (role code)	"Utility"	Navy
O (role code)	"Observation"	Navy
T (role code)	"Trainer"	Navy
A (maker code)	Brewster	Navy (Manufacturer Code)
B (maker code)	Beechcraft	Navy (Manufacturer Code)
C (maker code)	Curtiss	Navy (Manufacturer Code)
D (maker code)	Douglas	Navy (Manufacturer Code)
F (maker code)	Grumman	Navy (Manufacturer Code)
U (maker code)	Vought	Navy (Manufacturer Code)
V (maker code)	Lockheed	Navy (Manufacturer Code)
G (maker code)	Goodyear	Navy (Manufacturer Code)

M (maker code)	Martin	Navy (Manufacturer Code)
N (maker code)	Naval Aircraft Factory	Navy (Manufacturer Code)
P (role code)	"Pursuit" (Fighter)	Army
B (role code)	"Bomber"	Army
A (role code)	"Attack"	Army
C (role code)	"Cargo/Transport"	Army
L (role code)	"Liason"	Army
O (role code)	"Observation"	Army
T (role code)	"Trainer"	Army

ADDITIONAL INFORMATION ON WORLD WAR II AIRCRAFT DESIGNATIONS

Code Formats

Model Number: Occurring after the dash (Army), or in the middle of the three-letter prefix (Navy), it is the number assigned to a specific aircraft design to identify its place in a sequence of similar aircraft. In other words, it indicates which version of a design was accepted or submitted by the military within a specific aircraft category, such as fighter, bomber, or transport.

Variant Number (e.g., 2, 3, 25, etc.): Following a dash (Navy only), the last number in an aircraft's designation code represents the sequential order of factory or equipment design variations for that aircraft's role. Note: Army variant numbers omit the dash.

Variant Letter (e.g., A, B, C, etc.): Occurring after the model number (at the end of a designation code), the variant letter indicates specific model changes, updates, or improvements to an aircraft.

Example of a U.S. Army Air Forces aircraft, the North American P-51D-20-NA Mustang: P ("Pursuit") is the role prefix, 51 is the model number, D is the variant letter (4th major version), 20 is the block number denoting its specific production batch, NA (North American Aviation) is the factory code, and Mustang is the type name.

Other Role Codes

Additional role codes may include N for "Night Fighter," P for "Photo Reconnaissance," and K for "Drone."

INTRODUCTION

IT WAS MY GREAT PRIVILEGE to grow up in the post World War II era, a time when aircraft from that conflict were not only still popular, but were often still flown, many even which continued to be used by the military. The famed World War II transport aircraft, the C-47 Skytrain, for example, was employed by multiple branches of the military well into the 1970s, as was the P-51 Mustang, the Spitfire, and the B-25 Mitchell.

As a young artist and budding historian, naturally my own childhood was filled with plastic models of Warhawks, Corsairs, Messerschmitts, Zeroes, and B-17s, glamorous classic fighters that I spent endless hours gluing, painting, and admiring. Hanging them from my bedroom ceiling (using fishing line) allowed me an occasional glancing escape from the doldrums of homework. The pleasant memory of those wonderful model planes are etched into my memory, still clear even decades later.

My childhood reveries aside, we must never forget that the aerial machines featured in this book were responsible for incalculable destruction and bloodshed, and I have attempted to portray this very fact

in my illustrations. Yet, there is another side to them, one perhaps most appreciated by artists and designers such as myself. I am speaking of their sheer physical beauty. Similar to the designers behind the automotive industry of that era (the graceful 1942 Buick Roadmaster immediately comes to mind), aircraft engineers inadvertently created and produced some of the most elegant, attractive, and aesthetically pleasing planes the world has ever known, and it is to this aspect of World War II aircraft that much of this book is dedicated.

Above all my book honors The Greatest Generation, those born between 1901 and 1927, and who lived through the Great Depression and who fought in or supported World War II. Their stalwart patriotism, selfless courage, iron will, sterling character, and countless personal sacrifices made it possible for all subsequent generations—Baby Boomers, Generation X (X Geners), Millennials (Y Geners), Generation Z (Z Geners), and Generation Alpha—to live free and independent lives, unencumbered by the deadly threats and nihilistic influences of socialism and communism. Long may these hard-won freedoms continue! This book is my personal salute to those who made them possible.

Lochlainn Seabrook
Park County, Wyoming USA
August 2025
In Nobis Regnat Christus

The Avro Lancaster. Copyright © Lochlainn Seabrook.

SECTION ONE

United States Aircraft

1. P-51D MUSTANG

Static display, P-51D Mustang. Copyright © Lochlainn Seabrook.

AIRCRAFT PROFILE
Name: North American P-51D Mustang.
Country: United States.
Manufacturer: North American Aviation.
First Flight: October 26, 1940.
Primary Role: Long-range escort fighter.
Crew: 1.
Engine: Packard V-1650-7 (licensed Rolls-Royce Merlin V-12).
Top Speed: 437 mph.
Range: 1,650 miles (with external drop tanks).
Service Ceiling: 41,900 ft.
Armament: 6 × .50 cal M2 Browning machine guns; up to 2,000 lbs. of bombs or rockets.
Notable Use: Escorting B-17 and B-24 bombers deep into Nazi Germany; flown by elite U.S. fighter groups.

Training flight, P-51D Mustang. Copyright © Lochlainn Seabrook.

Cockpit view, P-51D Mustang. Copyright © Lochlainn Seabrook.

Combat scene, P-51D Mustang. Copyright © Lochlainn Seabrook.

2. B-17 FLYING FORTRESS

Static display, B-17 Flying Fortress. Copyright © Lochlainn Seabrook.

AIRCRAFT PROFILE

Name: B-17 Flying Fortress.
Country: United States.
Manufacturer: Boeing.
First Flight: July 28, 1935.
Primary Role: Heavy Bomber.
Crew: 10 (pilot, co-pilot, bombardier, navigator, radio operator, top turret gunner/engineer, ball turret gunner, two waist gunners, tail gunner).
Engine: 4 × Wright R-1820-97 Cyclone radial engines, 1,200 hp each.
Top Speed: 287 mph (at 25,000 ft).
Range: 2,000 miles (combat loaded).
Service Ceiling: 35,600 ft.
Armament: Up to 13 × .50 caliber (12.7 mm) M2 Browning machine guns in multiple defensive positions. Up to 8,000 lbs. of bombs (typical), with a maximum of 17,600 lbs. over short distances.
Notable Use: Iconic for its strategic daylight bombing raids over Nazi-occupied Europe. Played a key role in the U.S. Army Air Forces' air campaign against Germany. Known for absorbing heavy damage and still returning home, earning a legendary reputation for toughness. Participated in missions such as the Schweinfurt-Regensburg raid and the bombing of Berlin.

Training flight, B-17 Flying Fortress. Copyright © Lochlainn Seabrook.

Bombardier's compartment, B-17 Flying Fortress. Copyright © Lochlainn Seabrook.

Combat scene, B-17 Flying Fortress. Copyright © Lochlainn Seabrook.

3. F4U CORSAIR

Static display, F4U Corsair. Copyright © Lochlainn Seabrook.

AIRCRAFT PROFILE

Name: F4U Corsair.
Country: United States.
Manufacturer: Vought (also produced under license by Goodyear and Brewster).
First Flight: May 29, 1940.
Primary Role: Carrier-based Fighter/Fighter-Bomber.
Crew: 1.
Top Speed: 446 mph (at 26,200 ft).
Range: 1,015 miles (combat radius), 1,560 miles (ferry range).
Service Ceiling: 37,000 feet.
Armament: 6 × .50 caliber (12.7 mm) M2 Browning machine guns. Up to 4,000 lbs. of bombs or rockets (e.g., 8 × 5-inch rockets or 2 × 1,000 lb. bombs)
Notable Use: Famed for its combat success in the Pacific Theater during World War II, especially in the hands of U.S. Navy and Marine Corps pilots. The Corsair achieved one of the highest kill-to-loss ratios of the war and remained in frontline service through the Korean War. Its distinctive inverted gull-wing design and "Whistling Death" nickname made it an icon of American airpower.

Training flight, F4U Corsair. Copyright © Lochlainn Seabrook.

Frontal view, F4U Corsair. Copyright © Lochlainn Seabrook.

Combat scene, F4U Corsair. Copyright © Lochlainn Seabrook.

4. P-38 LIGHTNING

Static display, P-38 Lightning. Copyright © Lochlainn Seabrook.

AIRCRAFT PROFILE
Name: Lockheed P-38 Lightning.
Country: United States.
Manufacturer: Lockheed Corporation.
First Flight: January 27, 1939.
Primary Role: Long-range fighter, interceptor, fighter-bomber, reconnaissance.
Crew: 1.
Top Speed: 414 mph (at 25,000 ft).
Range: 1,300 miles (standard) up to 2,600 miles with drop tanks.
Service Ceiling: 44,000 ft.
Armament: 1 × 20 mm Hispano M2 cannon; 4 × .50 caliber (12.7 mm) Browning machine guns in the nose. Up to 4,000 lbs. of bombs or rockets on underwing hardpoints.
Notable Use: Famous as the aircraft flown by American national hero and top ace Richard Bong. Played a key role in the Pacific Theater, notably in Operation Vengeance, the mission to shoot down Japanese Admiral Isoroku Yamamoto in 1943. Extensively used for ground attack, bomber escort, and photo-reconnaissance missions across Europe, North Africa, and the Pacific.

Training flight, P-38 Lightning. Copyright © Lochlainn Seabrook.

Aft view of the empennage, P-38 Lightning. Copyright © Lochlainn Seabrook.

Combat scene, P-38 Lightning. Copyright © Lochlainn Seabrook.

5. B-29 SUPERFORTRESS

Static display, B-29 Superfortress. Copyright © Lochlainn Seabrook.

AIRCRAFT PROFILE
Name: B-29 Superfortress.
Country: United States.
Manufacturer: Boeing.
First Flight: September 21, 1942.
Primary Role: Strategic heavy bomber.
Crew: 11 (aircraft commander/pilot, co-pilot, bombardier, navigator, flight engineer, radio operator, radar operator, central fire control gunner, left gunner, right gunner, tail gunner).
Top Speed: 357 mph.
Range: 3,250 miles.
Service Ceiling: 31,850 feet.
Armament: Up to 12 × .50 caliber machine guns in remote-controlled turrets and tail, 1 × 20 mm cannon in tail (early models), and up to 20,000 lbs. of bombs.
Notable Use: Dropped atomic bombs on Hiroshima and Nagasaki in August 1945, ending World War II.

Training flight, B-29 Superfortress. Copyright © Lochlainn Seabrook.

Three-quarter nose view, B-29 Superfortress. Copyright © Lochlainn Seabrook.

Combat scene, B-29 Superfortress. Copyright © Lochlainn Seabrook.

6. P-47 THUNDERBOLT

Static display, P-47 Thunderbolt. Copyright © Lochlainn Seabrook.

AIRCRAFT PROFILE
Name: P-47 Thunderbolt.
Country: United States.
Manufacturer: Republic Aviation.
First Flight: May 6, 1941.
Primary Role: Fighter-bomber.
Crew: 1.
Top Speed: Approximately 433 mph (Mach 0.57) at 30,000 feet.
Range: Up to 1,800 miles with drop tanks.
Service Ceiling: 43,000 feet.
Armament: Eight .50 caliber M2 Browning machine guns; up to 2,500 lbs. of bombs or ten 5-inch rockets.
Notable Use: Used extensively in the European Theater during World War II for bomber escort and ground attack missions, including close air support during the Normandy invasion and the drive across France.

Training flight, P-47 Thunderbolt. Copyright © Lochlainn Seabrook.

Cockpit view, P-47 Thunderbolt. Copyright © Lochlainn Seabrook.

Combat scene, P-47 Thunderbolt. Copyright © Lochlainn Seabrook.

7. SBD DAUNTLESS

Static display, SBD Dauntless. Copyright © Lochlainn Seabrook.

AIRCRAFT PROFILE

Name: SBD Dauntless.
Country: United States.
Manufacturer: Douglas Aircraft Company.
First Flight: May 1, 1940.
Primary Role: Dive bomber.
Crew: 2 (pilot, rear gunner).
Top Speed: 255 mph.
Range: 1,115 miles.
Service Ceiling: 25,530 feet.
Armament: Two forward-firing 0.50 in machine guns, two rear-mounted 0.30 in machine guns, and up to 2,250 lbs. of bombs.
Notable Use: Credited with sinking four Japanese aircraft carriers at the Battle of Midway in June 1942, turning the tide of the Pacific War.

Training flight, SBD Dauntless. Copyright © Lochlainn Seabrook.

Engine maintenance scene, SBD Dauntless. Copyright © Lochlainn Seabrook.

Combat scene, SBD Dauntless. Copyright © Lochlainn Seabrook.

8. B-25 MITCHELL

Static display, B-25 Mitchell. Copyright © Lochlainn Seabrook.

AIRCRAFT PROFILE

Name: B-25 Mitchell.
Country: United States.
Manufacturer: North American Aviation.
First Flight: August 19, 1940.
Primary Role: Medium bomber.
Crew: 5 to 6 (pilot, co-pilot, navigator/bombardier, radio operator/gunner, flight engineer/top turret gunner, tail gunner).
Top Speed: Approximately 275 mph.
Range: Approximately 1,350 miles.
Service Ceiling: Approximately 24,200 feet.
Armament: Up to 13 × .50 caliber machine guns; up to 3,000 lbs. of bombs.
Notable Use: Most famous for the Doolittle Raid on Japan in April 1942, the first U.S. air raid to strike the Japanese home islands during World War II.

Training flight, B-25 Mitchell. Copyright © Lochlainn Seabrook.

Restored modern variant, B-25 Mitchell. Copyright © Lochlainn Seabrook.

Combat scene, B-25 Mitchell. Copyright © Lochlainn Seabrook.

9. C-47 SKYTRAIN

Static display, C-47 Skytrain. Copyright © Lochlainn Seabrook.

AIRCRAFT PROFILE

Name: C-47 Skytrain.
Country: United States.
Manufacturer: Douglas Aircraft Company.
First Flight: December 23, 1941 (military variant: DC-3 first flew December 17, 1935).
Primary Role: Military transport aircraft.
Crew: 3-6 (pilot, co-pilot, navigator, radio operator, crew chief/loadmaster, aerial engineer/flight mechanic).
Top Speed: 230 mph.
Range: 1,600 miles.
Service Ceiling: 24,000 feet.
Armament: None (typically unarmed).
Notable Use: Paratrooper drops on D-Day, supply drops over the Himalayas ("The Hump"), and medical evacuations throughout World War II.

Training flight, C-47 Skytrain. Copyright © Lochlainn Seabrook.

Oblique front quarter view, C-47 Skytrain. Copyright © Lochlainn Seabrook.

Combat scene, C-47 Skytrain. Copyright © Lochlainn Seabrook.

10. F6F HELLCAT

Static display, F6F Hellcat. Copyright © Lochlainn Seabrook.

AIRCRAFT PROFILE
Name: F6F Hellcat.
Country: United States.
Manufacturer: Grumman Aircraft Engineering Corporation.
First Flight: June 26, 1942.
Primary Role: Carrier-based fighter.
Crew: 1.
Top Speed: 380 mph.
Range: 1,090 miles.
Service Ceiling: 37,300 feet.
Armament: Six 0.50 in (12.7 mm) M2 Browning machine guns; up to 2,000 lbs. of bombs or six 5-inch rockets.
Notable Use: Dominated the Pacific Theater in WWII; credited with over 5,000 enemy aircraft kills and played a key role in securing U.S. air superiority during battles such as the Philippine Sea and Leyte Gulf.

Training flight, F6F Hellcat. Copyright © Lochlainn Seabrook.

Dynamic low front three-quarter view, F6F Hellcat. Copyright © Lochlainn Seabrook.

Combat scene, F6F Hellcat. Copyright © Lochlainn Seabrook.

11. A-20 HAVOC

Static display, A-20 Havoc. Copyright © Lochlainn Seabrook.

AIRCRAFT PROFILE

Name: A-20 Havoc.
Country: United States.
Manufacturer: Douglas Aircraft Company.
First Flight: October 26, 1938.
Primary Role: Light bomber and ground attack aircraft.
Crew: 3 (pilot, bombardier/navigator, gunner).
Top Speed: Approximately 317 mph.
Range: About 1,025 miles.
Service Ceiling: 23,700 feet.
Armament: Up to 6 × .50 cal machine guns in the nose, dorsal, and ventral positions; up to 4,000 lbs. of bombs.
Notable Use: Extensively used in low-level bombing and strafing missions during World War II in the European and Pacific Theaters by the U.S., U.K., Soviet Union, and other Allied forces.

Training flight, A-20 Havoc. Copyright © Lochlainn Seabrook.

Propeller and forward nacelle assembly view, A-20 Havoc. Copyright © Lochlainn Seabrook.

Combat scene, A-20 Havoc. Copyright © Lochlainn Seabrook.

12. PBY CATALINA

Static display, PBY Catalina. Copyright © Lochlainn Seabrook.

AIRCRAFT PROFILE

Name: PBY Catalina.
Country: United States.
Manufacturer: Consolidated Aircraft.
First Flight: March 28, 1935.
Primary Role: Maritime patrol, reconnaissance, search and rescue, and anti-submarine warfare.
Crew: 8 to 9 (pilot, co-pilot, navigator, bombardier, flight engineer, radio operator, bow gunner, waist gunner, tail gunner).
Top Speed: 196 mph.
Range: 2,520 miles.
Service Ceiling: 15,800 ft.
Armament: Up to five .30 cal. and .50 cal. machine guns; up to 4,000 lbs. of bombs, depth charges, or torpedoes.
Notable Use: Famous for long-range patrols in the Pacific Theater during World War II, the PBY Catalina was crucial in anti-submarine operations, maritime reconnaissance, air-sea rescue missions, and convoy escort duties. As an amphibious aircraft, it could land and take off from both runways and open water, making it indispensable for search and rescue missions—especially the recovery of downed airmen in remote oceanic theaters.

Training flight, PBY Catalina. Copyright © Lochlainn Seabrook.

Cockpit oblique interior view, PBY Catalina. Copyright © Lochlainn Seabrook.

Combat scene, PBY Catalina. Copyright © Lochlainn Seabrook.

13. TBF AVENGER

Static display, TBF Avenger. Copyright © Lochlainn Seabrook.

AIRCRAFT PROFILE
Name: TBF Avenger.
Country: United States.
Manufacturer: Grumman Aircraft Engineering Corporation.
First Flight: August 7, 1941.
Primary Role: Torpedo bomber.
Crew: 3 (pilot, turret gunner, radioman/bombardier/ventral gunner).
Top Speed: 275 mph.
Range: 1,000 miles.
Service Ceiling: 30,100 ft.
Armament: One 0.50 in. machine gun in a powered dorsal turret, one 0.30 in. machine gun in a ventral position, one fixed forward-firing 0.30 or 0.50 in. machine gun in the nose, and up to 2,000 lbs. of bombs or a Mark 13 torpedo.
Notable Use: Played a decisive role in the Battle of Midway, the Battle of the Philippine Sea, and throughout the Pacific Theater. Famously flown by future U.S. President George H. W. Bush during World War II.

Training flight, TBF Avenger. Copyright © Lochlainn Seabrook.

Three-quarter front cockpit view, TBF Avenger. Copyright © Lochlainn Seabrook.

Combat scene, TBF Avenger. Copyright © Lochlainn Seabrook.

14. B-24 LIBERATOR

Static display, B-24 Liberator. Copyright © Lochlainn Seabrook.

AIRCRAFT PROFILE

Name: B-24 Liberator.
Country: United States.
Manufacturer: Consolidated Aircraft.
First Flight: December 29, 1939.
Primary Role: Heavy bomber.
Crew: 10 (pilot, co-pilot, navigator, bombardier, flight engineer/top turret gunner, radio operator, nose gunner, waist gunner—port, waist gunner—starboard, tail gunner).
Top Speed: 290 mph.
Range: 2,100 miles (standard bomb load); up to 3,700 miles with auxiliary fuel tanks.
Service Ceiling: 28,000 ft.
Armament: Up to 10 × .50 cal. M2 Browning machine guns in nose, tail, dorsal, ventral, and waist positions; up to 8,000 lbs. of bombs internally.
Notable Use: Served in every theater of World War II; known for long-range missions, including anti-submarine warfare in the Atlantic and strategic bombing over Europe and the Pacific; played a key role in missions such as Operation Tidal Wave against oil refineries in Ploieşt, Romania.

Training flight, B-24 Liberator. Copyright © Lochlainn Seabrook.

Left front quarter view, B-24 Liberator. Copyright © Lochlainn Seabrook.

Combat scene, B-24 Liberator. Copyright © Lochlainn Seabrook.

15. F2A BUFFALO

Static display, F2A Buffalo. Copyright © Lochlainn Seabrook.

AIRCRAFT PROFILE

Name: F2A Buffalo.
Country: United States.
Manufacturer: Brewster Aeronautical Corporation.
First Flight: December 2, 1937.
Primary Role: Carrier-based fighter.
Crew: 1.
Top Speed: 321 mph at 16,500 ft.
Range: 965 miles.
Service Ceiling: 32,000 ft.
Armament: One 0.50 in. M2 Browning machine gun and one 0.30 in. M1919 Browning machine gun in the nose (early variants); up to four 0.50 in. M2 Browning machine guns in later variants. Some versions could also carry two 100 lb. bombs under the wings.
Notable Use: Despite poor performance in the Pacific Theater, the F2A Buffalo achieved notable success with the Finnish Air Force against the Soviet Union during the Continuation War (1941–1944), where it was praised for its ruggedness and kill ratio. The Navy's first monoplane fighter to be deployed on aircraft carriers, it was eventually deemed inadequate for carrier warfare. Relegated to training and land-based roles, it later saw its most effective combat use with allied air forces.

Training flight, F2A Buffalo. Copyright © Lochlainn Seabrook.

Left front quarter view, F2A Buffalo. Copyright © Lochlainn Seabrook.

Combat scene, F2A Buffalo. Copyright © Lochlainn Seabrook.

16. P-39 AIRACOBRA

Static display, P-39 Airacobra. Copyright © Lochlainn Seabrook.

AIRCRAFT PROFILE
Name: P-39 Airacobra.
Country: United States.
Manufacturer: Bell Aircraft Corporation.
First Flight: April 6, 1938.
Primary Role: Fighter.
Crew: 1.
Top Speed: Approximately 385 mph at 15,000 ft.
Range: Approximately 600 miles.
Service Ceiling: 35,000 ft.
Armament: One 37 mm T9 cannon firing through the propeller hub, two synchronized .50 cal. machine guns in the nose, and four .30 cal. machine guns in the wings (later versions often replaced wing guns with .50 cal. units).
Notable Use: Widely used by the Soviet Air Force under Lend-Lease during World War II, where it achieved significant success in low- to mid-altitude combat. Also employed by the U.S. Army Air Forces in the Pacific and Mediterranean theaters, though with less acclaim due to performance limitations at high altitudes.

Training flight, P-39 Airacobra. Copyright © Lochlainn Seabrook.

Three-quarter cockpit view, P-39 Airacobra. Copyright © Lochlainn Seabrook.

Combat scene, P-39 Airacobra. Copyright © Lochlainn Seabrook.

17. P-40 WARHAWK

Static display, P-40 Warhawk. Copyright © Lochlainn Seabrook.

AIRCRAFT PROFILE
Name: P-40 Warhawk.
Country: United States.
Manufacturer: Curtiss-Wright Corporation.
First Flight: October 14, 1938.
Primary Role: Fighter and ground-attack aircraft.
Crew: 1.
Top Speed: Approximately 360 mph.
Range: Approximately 650 miles.
Service Ceiling: Approximately 29,000 ft.
Armament: Six .50 caliber (12.7 mm) M2 Browning machine guns; up to 700 lbs. of bombs.
Notable Use: Famously flown by the American Volunteer Group, known as the "Flying Tigers," during combat operations against the Japanese in China and Burma in World War II.

Training flight, P-40 Warhawk. Copyright © Lochlainn Seabrook.

Oblique nose close-up, P-40 Warhawk. Copyright © Lochlainn Seabrook.

Combat scene, P-40 Warhawk. Copyright © Lochlainn Seabrook.

18. F4F WILDCAT

Static display, F4F Wildcat. Copyright © Lochlainn Seabrook.

AIRCRAFT PROFILE
Name: F4F Wildcat.
Country: United States.
Manufacturer: Grumman Aircraft Engineering Corporation.
First Flight: September 2, 1937.
Primary Role: Carrier-based fighter.
Crew: 1.
Top Speed: Approximately 331 mph at 21,000 ft.
Range: Approximately 845 miles.
Service Ceiling: Approximately 34,800 ft.
Armament: Four to six 0.50 in. (12.7 mm) Browning M2 machine guns, and two 100 lb. or 250 lb. bombs or six 5 in. High-Velocity Aircraft Rockets (HVARs) on later variants.
Notable Use: The F4F Wildcat was the primary U.S. Navy and Marine Corps fighter in the early years of World War II, notably serving during the Battles of Coral Sea, Midway, and Guadalcanal. Despite being outmatched in speed and maneuverability by the Japanese Mitsubishi A6M Zero, it was rugged, heavily armed, and exceptionally durable, earning a reputation for being able to take significant damage and still return to base.

Training flight, F4F Wildcat. Copyright © Lochlainn Seabrook.

Oblique close-up of prop hub, F4F Wildcat. Copyright © Lochlainn Seabrook.

Combat scene, F4F Wildcat. Copyright © Lochlainn Seabrook.

SECTION TWO

United Kingdom Aircraft

19. SUPERMARINE SPITFIRE

Static display, Supermarine Spitfire. Copyright © Lochlainn Seabrook.

AIRCRAFT PROFILE

Name: Supermarine Spitfire.
Country: United Kingdom.
Manufacturer: Supermarine Aviation Works (Vickers).
First Flight: March 5, 1936.
Primary Role: Fighter.
Crew: 1.
Top Speed: Approximately 370 mph (Spitfire Mk V at 19,500 ft).
Range: Up to 991 miles with drop tanks.
Service Ceiling: Approximately 36,500 ft.
Armament: Typically 2 × 20 mm Hispano Mk II cannons and 4 × .303 in Browning machine guns; later variants carried 4 × 20 mm cannons or 2 × 20 mm and 2 × .50 cal Browning machine guns, with optional underwing bombs.
Notable Use: Served in every major theater of WWII, famously defending Britain during the Battle of Britain, and later used in reconnaissance, ground attack, and escort roles; known for its elliptical wing design and superb agility.

Training flight, Supermarine Spitfire. Copyright © Lochlainn Seabrook.

Oblique close-up of cockpit canopy, Supermarine Spitfire. Copyright © Lochlainn Seabrook.

Combat scene, Supermarine Spitfire. Copyright © Lochlainn Seabrook.

20. AVRO LANCASTER

Static display, Avro Lancaster. Copyright © Lochlainn Seabrook.

AIRCRAFT PROFILE
Name: Avro Lancaster.
Country: United Kingdom.
Manufacturer: Avro (A.V. Roe and Company, Ltd.).
First Flight: January 9, 1941.
Primary Role: Heavy bomber.
Crew: 7 (pilot, flight engineer, navigator, bomb aimer/nose gunner, wireless operator, mid-upper gunner, tail gunner).
Top Speed: Approximately 287 mph.
Range: Approximately 2,530 miles.
Service Ceiling: Approximately 24,500 ft.
Armament: Up to 14,000 lbs. of bombs internally in standard configuration, with a maximum overload bomb load of 22,000 lbs.; eight 0.303 in. Browning machine guns (two in the nose turret, two in the dorsal turret, and four in the tail turret).
Notable Use: Best known for its pivotal role in the RAF's night bombing campaign over Germany, including the famous Operation Chastise ("Dambuster Raids") of 1943 using specially designed bouncing bombs against German dams.

Training flight, Avro Lancaster. Copyright © Lochlainn Seabrook.

Left rear quarter view, Avro Lancaster. Copyright © Lochlainn Seabrook.

Combat scene, Avro Lancaster. Copyright © Lochlainn Seabrook.

21. HAWKER HURRICANE

Static display, Hawker Hurricane. Copyright © Lochlainn Seabrook.

AIRCRAFT PROFILE
Name: Hawker Hurricane.
Country: United Kingdom.
Manufacturer: Hawker Aircraft Ltd.
First Flight: November 6, 1935.
Primary Role: Fighter.
Crew: 1.
Top Speed: Approximately 340 mph at 22,000 ft.
Range: Approximately 460 miles.
Service Ceiling: Approximately 36,000 ft.
Armament: Eight 0.303 in. (7.7 mm) Browning machine guns in early variants; later variants included two 20 mm Hispano cannons and the ability to carry bombs or rockets.
Notable Use: The Hurricane was the RAF's workhorse during the early years of World War II and was responsible for approximately 60 percent of all German aircraft downed during the Battle of Britain. It also served in North Africa, the Soviet Union, and the Far East.

Training flight, Hawker Hurricane. Copyright © Lochlainn Seabrook.

Right front quarter view, Hawker Hurricane. Copyright © Lochlainn Seabrook.

Combat scene, Hawker Hurricane. Copyright © Lochlainn Seabrook.

22. DE HAVILLAND MOSQUITO

Static display, De Havilland Mosquito. Copyright © Lochlainn Seabrook.

AIRCRAFT PROFILE
Name: De Havilland Mosquito.
Country: United Kingdom.
Manufacturer: De Havilland Aircraft Company.
First Flight: November 25, 1940.
Primary Role: Multi-role combat aircraft (fighter-bomber, reconnaissance, night fighter, pathfinder, and light bomber).
Crew: 2 (pilot, navigator/bombardier).
Top Speed: Approximately 415 mph.
Range: Approximately 1,500 miles.
Service Ceiling: 37,000 feet.
Armament: 4 × 20 mm Hispano Mk II cannons; 4 × .303 in Browning machine guns. Up to 4,000 lbs. of bombs or rockets (depending on variant).
Notable Use: Widely used by the RAF and allied air forces during World War II for precision strikes, night bombing, and photo reconnaissance missions. Famous for its all-wood construction, high speed, and versatility, the Mosquito earned the nickname "The Wooden Wonder."

Training flight, De Havilland Mosquito. Copyright © Lochlainn Seabrook.

Oblique undercarriage detail view, De Havilland Mosquito. Copyright © Lochlainn Seabrook.

Combat scene, De Havilland Mosquito. Copyright © Lochlainn Seabrook.

23. FAIREY SWORDFISH

Taxi-out phase, Fairey Swordfish. Copyright © Lochlainn Seabrook.

AIRCRAFT PROFILE

Name: Fairey Swordfish.
Country: United Kingdom.
Manufacturer: Fairey Aviation Company.
First Flight: April 17, 1934.
Primary Role: Torpedo bomber.
Crew: 3 (pilot, observer/navigator, telegraphist/air gunner).
Top Speed: 139 mph.
Range: 546 miles.
Service Ceiling: 10,700 ft.
Armament: One fixed forward-firing .303 in Vickers machine gun, one .303 in Lewis or Vickers K machine gun in the rear cockpit, and up to 1,500 lbs. of bombs or one 1,670 lb. torpedo.
Notable Use: Famously used by the Royal Navy Fleet Air Arm in the attack on the Italian fleet at Taranto in 1940 and the crippling of the German battleship Bismarck in 1941. Its outdated design proved effective in naval operations due to its ability to operate from aircraft carriers and escort ships in all weather conditions.

Training flight, Fairey Swordfish. Copyright © Lochlainn Seabrook.

Oblique close-up view of cockpit, Fairey Swordfish. Copyright © Lochlainn Seabrook.

Combat scene, Fairey Swordfish. Copyright © Lochlainn Seabrook.

24. GLOSTER GLADIATOR

Static display, Gloster Gladiator. Copyright © Lochlainn Seabrook.

AIRCRAFT PROFILE

Name: Gloster Gladiator.
Country: United Kingdom.
Manufacturer: Gloster Aircraft Company.
First Flight: September 12, 1934.
Primary Role: Fighter.
Crew: 1.
Top Speed: 257 mph.
Range: 444 miles.
Service Ceiling: 32,800 ft.
Armament: Four .303 in. (7.7 mm) Browning machine guns.
Notable Use: The Gloster Gladiator was the last biplane fighter used by the Royal Air Force and saw combat during the early years of World War II, including notable service in Norway, the Mediterranean, and the defense of Malta where the aircraft named "Faith," "Hope," and "Charity" became legendary symbols of resistance.

Training flight, Gloster Gladiator. Copyright © Lochlainn Seabrook.

Three-quarter front view of engine, Gloster Gladiator. Copyright © Lochlainn Seabrook.

Combat scene, Gloster Gladiator. Copyright © Lochlainn Seabrook.

25. BRISTOL BEAUFIGHTER

Static display, Bristol Beaufighter. Copyright © Lochlainn Seabrook.

AIRCRAFT PROFILE
Name: Bristol Beaufighter.
Country: United Kingdom.
Manufacturer: Bristol Aeroplane Company.
First Flight: July 17, 1939.
Primary Role: Heavy fighter and ground attack.
Crew: 2 (pilot, navigator/radar operator).
Top Speed: 320 mph.
Range: 1,500 miles.
Service Ceiling: 26,000 feet.
Armament: Four 20 mm Hispano cannons in the nose, six .303 in. machine guns in the wings (early variants), and external loadouts including bombs, torpedoes, or eight 3 in. rockets.
Notable Use: Used extensively by the RAF in night-fighter, anti-shipping, and ground-attack roles, including major operations in the Mediterranean, Burma, and the Battle of the Atlantic.

Training flight, Bristol Beaufighter. Copyright © Lochlainn Seabrook.

Oblique instrument panel view, Bristol Beaufighter. Copyright © Lochlainn Seabrook.

Combat scene, Bristol Beaufighter. Copyright © Lochlainn Seabrook.

26. SHORT SUNDERLAND

Static display, Short Sunderland. Copyright © Lochlainn Seabrook.

AIRCRAFT PROFILE

Name: Short Sunderland.
Country: United Kingdom.
Manufacturer: Short Brothers.
First Flight: October 16, 1937.
Primary Role: Long-range maritime patrol and anti-submarine warfare flying boat.
Crew: 7 to 11, depending on variant and mission profile (pilot, co-pilot, navigator, flight engineer, radio operator, bomb aimer, nose gunner, dorsal gunner, tail gunner, waist gunner—port, waist gunner—starboard.
Top Speed: Approximately 210 mph.
Range: 1,780 miles.
Service Ceiling: 16,400 ft.
Armament: Up to 16,000 lbs. of bombs, depth charges, or mines; up to 18 × .303 in. (7.7 mm) Browning machine guns in nose, dorsal, tail, and beam positions. Later variants equipped with 2 × .50 in. (12.7 mm) machine guns.
Notable Use: The Short Sunderland was one of the most important Allied flying boats of World War II, famed for its U-boat hunting success during the Battle of the Atlantic. Its heavy defensive armament earned it the nickname "The Flying Porcupine." It was an authentic flying boat, designed for sea operations only, with no land-based takeoff or landing ability in its wartime military form. It served extensively with RAF Coastal Command and Allied forces for anti-submarine patrols, convoy escort, reconnaissance, and air-sea rescue.

Training flight, Short Sunderland. Copyright © Lochlainn Seabrook.

Restored modern variant, Short Sunderland. Copyright © Lochlainn Seabrook.

Combat scene, Short Sunderland. Copyright © Lochlainn Seabrook.

SECTION THREE

German Aircraft

27. MESSERSCHMITT BF 109

Static display, Messerschmitt Bf 109. Copyright © Lochlainn Seabrook.

AIRCRAFT PROFILE
Name: Messerschmitt Bf 109.
Country: Germany.
Manufacturer: Bayerische Flugzeugwerke (later Messerschmitt AG).
First Flight: May 29, 1935.
Primary Role: Fighter.
Crew: 1.
Top Speed: Approximately 398 mph (640 km/h).
Range: Approximately 528 miles (850 km).
Service Ceiling: Approximately 39,370 ft.
Armament: Typically 2 × 13 mm MG 131 machine guns, 1 × 20 mm or 30 mm cannon, with various combinations depending on the variant.
Notable Use: Germany's most-produced fighter aircraft of World War II; flown by many of the Luftwaffe's top aces, including Erich Hartmann, the highest-scoring fighter ace in history with 352 aerial victories.

Training flight, Messerschmitt Bf 109. Copyright © Lochlainn Seabrook.

Restored modern variant, Messerschmitt Bf 109. Copyright © Lochlainn Seabrook.

Combat scene, Messerschmitt Bf 109. Copyright © Lochlainn Seabrook.

28. FOCKE-WULF FW 190

Static display, Focke-Wulf Fw 190. Copyright © Lochlainn Seabrook.

AIRCRAFT PROFILE
Name: Focke-Wulf Fw 190.
Country: Germany.
Manufacturer: Focke-Wulf Flugzeugbau AG.
First Flight: June 1, 1939.
Primary Role: Fighter and fighter-bomber.
Crew: 1.
Top Speed: Approximately 426 mph at 20,000 ft. (Fw 190 A-8 variant).
Range: Approximately 500 miles (combat radius), extendable to 560 miles with drop tanks.
Service Ceiling: Approximately 37,400 ft.
Armament: Typically 2 × 13 mm MG 131 machine guns, 4 × 20 mm MG 151/20 cannons, and up to 2,200 lbs. of bombs or air-to-ground rockets depending on variant.
Notable Use: Served as one of the Luftwaffe's premier fighters during World War II, excelling in air superiority, ground attack, and bomber interception roles. It was widely used on both the Eastern and Western fronts and considered a formidable adversary to Allied fighters such as the Spitfire and P-51 Mustang.

Training flight, Focke-Wulf Fw 190. Copyright © Lochlainn Seabrook.

Takeoff view, Focke-Wulf Fw 190. Copyright © Lochlainn Seabrook.

Combat scene, Focke-Wulf Fw 190. Copyright © Lochlainn Seabrook.

29. MESSERSCHMITT ME 262

Static display, Messerschmitt Me 262. Copyright © Lochlainn Seabrook.

AIRCRAFT PROFILE
Name: Messerschmitt Me 262.
Country: Germany.
Manufacturer: Messerschmitt AG.
First Flight: April 18, 1941.
Primary Role: Jet fighter and fighter-bomber.
Crew: 1.
Top Speed: Approximately 540 mph.
Range: Approximately 650 miles.
Service Ceiling: 37,500 ft.
Armament: Four 30 mm MK 108 cannons in the nose; optional 24 × R4M rockets or two 1,100 lb. bombs under the wings.
Notable Use: The Me 262 was the world's first operational jet-powered fighter aircraft, entering service in 1944. It was faster and more heavily armed than any Allied aircraft of the time, but limited production, fuel shortages, and pilot training constraints reduced its overall impact. It saw action primarily in interceptor and ground-attack roles, and was feared for its speed and firepower.

Training flight, Messerschmitt Me 262. Copyright © Lochlainn Seabrook.

Takeoff rotation view, Messerschmitt Me 262. Copyright © Lochlainn Seabrook.

Combat scene, Messerschmitt Me 262. Copyright © Lochlainn Seabrook.

30. JUNKERS JU 87 STUKA

Static display, Junkers Ju 87 Stuka. Copyright © Lochlainn Seabrook.

AIRCRAFT PROFILE
Name: Junkers Ju 87 Stuka.
Country: Germany.
Manufacturer: Junkers Flugzeug- und Motorenwerke AG.
First Flight: September 17, 1935.
Primary Role: Dive bomber and ground-attack aircraft.
Crew: 2 (pilot, rear gunner).
Top Speed: Approximately 255 mph.
Range: Approximately 300 miles with standard bomb load.
Service Ceiling: Approximately 26,250 ft.
Armament: Two 7.92 mm MG 17 machine guns forward, one 7.92 mm MG 15 or MG 81Z rearward, and up to 3,970 lbs. of bombs, depending on variant.
Notable Use: Widely used during the early stages of World War II, especially during the invasions of Poland, France, and the Low Countries, the Ju 87 became infamous for its screaming dive-bombing sirens and psychological impact, playing a key role in Germany's Blitzkrieg operations.

Training flight, Junkers Ju 87 Stuka. Copyright © Lochlainn Seabrook.

Restored modern variant, Junkers Ju 87 Stuka. Copyright © Lochlainn Seabrook.

Combat scene, Junkers Ju 87 Stuka. Copyright © Lochlainn Seabrook.

31. HEINKEL HE 111

Static display, Heinkel He 111. Copyright © Lochlainn Seabrook.

AIRCRAFT PROFILE
Name: Heinkel He 111.
Country: Germany.
Manufacturer: Heinkel Flugzeugwerke.
First Flight: February 24, 1935.
Primary Role: Medium bomber.
Crew: 5 (pilot, co-pilot, navigator/bombardier, radio operator/rear gunner, dorsal gunner).
Top Speed: Approximately 273 mph.
Range: Approximately 1,420 miles.
Service Ceiling: Approximately 27,560 ft.
Armament: Up to 7 × 7.92 mm MG 15 or MG 81 machine guns; internal bomb load of up to 4,400 lbs.; external bomb racks could carry up to 4,400 additional lbs., depending on configuration.
Notable Use: Served as the Luftwaffe's primary strategic bomber during the early years of World War II, including in the Battle of Britain, the Blitz, and campaigns in Poland, France, and the Soviet Union.

Training flight, Heinkel He 111. Copyright © Lochlainn Seabrook.

Landing rotation, three-quarter front view, Heinkel He 111. Copyright © Lochlainn Seabrook.

Combat scene, Heinkel He 111. Copyright © Lochlainn Seabrook.

32. DORNIER DO 17

Static display, Dornier Do 17. Copyright © Lochlainn Seabrook.

AIRCRAFT PROFILE
Name: Dornier Do 17.
Country: Germany.
Manufacturer: Dornier Flugzeugwerke.
First Flight: 1934.
Primary Role: Light bomber and reconnaissance aircraft.
Crew: 4 (pilot, navigator/bombardier, radio operator/rear gunner, nose gunner).
Top Speed: 255 mph.
Range: 720 miles.
Service Ceiling: 26,000 ft.
Armament: Typically 3 to 6 × 7.92 mm MG 15 machine guns; up to 2,200 lbs. of bombs.
Notable Use: Extensively used by the Luftwaffe during the early years of World War II, including the Invasion of Poland, the Battle of France, and the Battle of Britain. Known as the "Flying Pencil" due to its slim fuselage design.

Training flight, Dornier Do 17. Copyright © Lochlainn Seabrook.

Three-quarter front underside view, Dornier Do 17. Copyright © Lochlainn Seabrook.

Combat scene, Dornier Do 17. Copyright © Lochlainn Seabrook.

33. ARADO AR 234

Static display, Arado Ar 234 Blitz. Copyright © Lochlainn Seabrook.

AIRCRAFT PROFILE
Name: Arado Ar 234 Blitz.
Country: Germany.
Manufacturer: Arado Flugzeugwerke.
First Flight: June 15, 1943.
Primary Role: Jet-powered reconnaissance bomber.
Crew: 1.
Top Speed: 461 mph.
Range: 1,000 miles.
Service Ceiling: 32,800 ft.
Armament: Two 20 mm MG 151/20 cannons (optional on later versions). Up to 3,300 lbs. of bombs carried externally or in a central bomb bay.
Notable Use: The Ar 234 was the world's first operational jet-powered bomber, used by the Luftwaffe for high-speed reconnaissance and precision bombing missions late in World War II, including operations over Normandy, the Ardennes, and the Western Front.

Training flight, Arado Ar 234 Blitz. Copyright © Lochlainn Seabrook.

Restored modern variant, Arado Ar 234 Blitz. Copyright © Lochlainn Seabrook.

Combat scene, Arado Ar 234 Blitz. Copyright © Lochlainn Seabrook.

34. MESSERSCHMITT BF 110

Static display, Messerschmitt Bf 110. Copyright © Lochlainn Seabrook.

AIRCRAFT PROFILE

Name: Messerschmitt Bf 110.
Country: Germany.
Manufacturer: Bayerische Flugzeugwerke (Messerschmitt AG).
First Flight: May 12, 1936.
Primary Role: Heavy fighter (Zerstörer), fighter-bomber, night fighter.
Crew: 2–3 (pilot, rear gunner/radio operator, and optional radar operator in later variants).
Top Speed: Approximately 336 mph.
Range: Up to 680 miles.
Service Ceiling: Approximately 32,800 ft.
Armament: Typically included 2 × 20 mm MG FF/M cannons, 4 × 7.92 mm MG 17 machine guns in the nose, 1 × 7.92 mm MG 15 or MG 81Z rear defensive gun, and up to 2,200 lbs. of bombs or underwing rockets depending on the variant.
Notable Use: Widely used by the Luftwaffe during the early stages of World War II in the invasions of Poland, France, and the Low Countries, and later adapted as an effective night fighter during the Defense of the Reich, particularly when equipped with radar and Schräge Musik upward-firing cannons.

Training flight, Messerschmitt Bf 110. Copyright © Lochlainn Seabrook.

Takeoff rotation view, Messerschmitt Bf 110. Copyright © Lochlainn Seabrook.

Combat scene, Messerschmitt Bf 110. Copyright © Lochlainn Seabrook.

35. FIESELER FI 156 STORCH

Static display, Fieseler Fi 156 Storch. Copyright © Lochlainn Seabrook.

AIRCRAFT PROFILE
Name: Fieseler Fi 156 Storch.
Country: Germany.
Manufacturer: Fieseler Flugzeugbau.
First Flight: May 1936.
Primary Role: Liaison and reconnaissance aircraft.
Crew: 2 to 3 (pilot, observer, rear gunner).
Top Speed: 109 mph.
Range: 239 miles.
Service Ceiling: 15,420 ft.
Armament: One 7.92 mm MG 15 machine gun in rear cockpit (some variants unarmed).
Notable Use: The Fi 156 Storch was renowned for its extraordinary short takeoff and landing (STOL) capability. It was used extensively by the Luftwaffe for battlefield observation, medical evacuation, and liaison missions. One of its most famous missions was the daring 1943 rescue of deposed Italian dictator Benito Mussolini from a mountaintop hotel during Operation Eiche. Primary functions: battlefield reconnaissance, artillery spotting, liaison duties, medical evacuation, and command transport.

Training flight, Fieseler Fi 156 Storch. Copyright © Lochlainn Seabrook.

Restored modern variant, Fieseler Fi 156 Storch. Copyright © Lochlainn Seabrook.

Combat rescue scene, Fieseler Fi 156 Storch. Copyright © Lochlainn Seabrook.

36. JUNKERS JU 88

Static display, Junkers Ju 88. Copyright © Lochlainn Seabrook.

AIRCRAFT PROFILE

Name: Junkers Ju 88.
Country: Germany.
Manufacturer: Junkers Flugzeug- und Motorenwerke AG.
First Flight: December 21, 1936.
Primary Role: Multi-role combat aircraft (bomber, night fighter, reconnaissance, and more).
Crew: 4 (pilot, navigator/bombardier, radio operator/rear gunner, dorsal gunner).
Top Speed: 292 mph at 18,000 ft.
Range: 1,500 miles.
Service Ceiling: 26,900 ft.
Armament: Up to 13 × 7.92 mm MG 15 machine guns or 20 mm MG FF/M cannons, plus up to 6,600 lbs. of bombs internally and externally.
Notable Use: Extensively deployed by the Luftwaffe throughout World War II in nearly every major theater of the European conflict; served as a versatile platform for level bombing, dive bombing, ground attack, anti-shipping missions, and night fighting.

Training flight, Junkers Ju 88. Copyright © Lochlainn Seabrook.

Takeoff rotation view, Junkers Ju 88. Copyright © Lochlainn Seabrook.

Combat scene, Junker Ju 88. Copyright © Lochlainn Seabrook.

SECTION ONE

Japanese Aircraft

37. MITSUBISHI A6M ZERO

Static display, Mitsubishi A6M Zero. Copyright © Lochlainn Seabrook.

AIRCRAFT PROFILE

Name: Mitsubishi A6M Zero.
Country: Japan.
Manufacturer: Mitsubishi Heavy Industries.
First Flight: April 1, 1939.
Primary Role: Carrier-based fighter.
Crew: 1.
Top Speed: Approximately 351 mph.
Range: Approximately 1,930 miles.
Service Ceiling: Approximately 33,000 ft.
Armament: Two 7.7 mm Type 97 machine guns, two 20 mm Type 99 cannons, and up to 132 lbs. of bombs.
Notable Use: Dominated early Pacific air battles in World War II, including the attack on Pearl Harbor and the Battle of the Coral Sea. Feared for its agility and range, it was eventually outclassed by more advanced Allied aircraft.

Training flight, Mitsubishi A6M Zero. Copyright © Lochlainn Seabrook.

Restored modern variant, Mitsubishi A6M Zero. Copyright © Lochlainn Seabrook.

Combat scene, Mitsubishi A6M Zero. Copyright © Lochlainn Seabrook.

38. NAKAJIMA KI-43 "OSCAR"

Static display, Nakajima Ki-43. Copyright © Lochlainn Seabrook.

AIRCRAFT PROFILE

Name: Nakajima Ki-43 "Oscar."
Country: Japan.
Manufacturer: Nakajima Aircraft Company.
First Flight: January 1939.
Primary Role: Fighter.
Crew: 1.
Top Speed: Approximately 329 mph at 13,125 ft.
Range: Approximately 1,090 miles.
Service Ceiling: Approximately 36,750 ft.
Armament: Typically two 12.7 mm Ho-103 machine guns. Some later variants carried one 20 mm cannon and one 12.7 mm machine gun. The aircraft could also carry two 551 lb. bombs.
Notable Use: The Ki-43 was the most widely used Japanese Army fighter of World War II, known for its exceptional maneuverability. It served extensively in China, Southeast Asia, the Pacific, and Burma. Allied pilots often underestimated it, but skilled Japanese aces used the Oscar to great effect in dogfights. Despite its light armor and limited firepower, it remained in front-line service through the war due to its agility and ease of production. "Oscar," still the common Western intelligence reference for the Nakajima Ki-43, was part of the Allied naming system—a codename intended to help Allied pilots identify Japanese aircraft.

Training flight, Nakajima Ki-43. Copyright © Lochlainn Seabrook.

Restored modern variant, Nakajima Ki-43. Copyright © Lochlainn Seabrook.

Combat scene, Nakajima Ki-43. Copyright © Lochlainn Seabrook.

39. KAWANISHI H8K "EMILY"

Static display, Kawanishi H8K. Copyright © Lochlainn Seabrook.

AIRCRAFT PROFILE
Name: Kawanishi H8K "Emily."
Country: Japan.
Manufacturer: Kawanishi Aircraft Company.
First Flight: January 1941.
Primary Role: Long-range maritime patrol bomber and reconnaissance flying boat.
Crew: 10 (pilot, co-pilot, navigator, flight engineer, radio operator, nose gunner, dorsal gunner, tail gunner, waist gunner—port, waist gunner—starboard).
Top Speed: 296 mph.
Range: 4,460 miles.
Service Ceiling: 28,000 ft.
Armament: Up to 5 × 20 mm Type 99 cannons; 4 × 7.7 mm Type 92 machine guns. Up to 2,200 lbs. of bombs or 2 × 1,764 lb. torpedoes.
Notable Use: Widely regarded as one of the best flying boats of World War II, the H8K gained a reputation for its durability, long range, and heavy defensive armament. It participated in night raids such as the second attack on Pearl Harbor (March 1942), conducted extensive reconnaissance missions across the Pacific, and was feared by Allied forces for its combat resilience and reach. "Emily," still the common Western intelligence reference for the Kawanishi H8K, was part of the Allied naming system—a codename intended to help Allied pilots identify Japanese aircraft.

Training flight, Kawanishi H8K. Copyright © Lochlainn Seabrook.

Head-on waterborne rotation view, Kawanishi H8K. Copyright © Lochlainn Seabrook.

Combat scene, Kawanishi H8K. Copyright © Lochlainn Seabrook.

40. YOKOSUKA D4Y "JUDY"

Static display, Yokosuka D4Y. Copyright © Lochlainn Seabrook.

AIRCRAFT PROFILE

Name: Yokosuka D4Y "Judy."
Country: Japan.
Manufacturer: Yokosuka Naval Air Technical Arsenal.
First Flight: December 1940.
Primary Role: Carrier-based dive bomber and reconnaissance aircraft.
Crew: 2 (pilot, radio operator/rear gunner).
Top Speed: 342 mph.
Range: 915 miles.
Service Ceiling: 35,000 ft.
Armament: Two 7.7 mm Type 97 machine guns in the nose, one flexible 7.92 mm machine gun in the rear cockpit, and up to 1,102 lbs. of bombs (typically one 1,102 lb. bomb or one 550 lb. bomb and two 132 lb. bombs).
Notable Use: Widely deployed by the Imperial Japanese Navy from 1942 to 1945, including during the battles of the Philippine Sea and Leyte Gulf. Later versions were used in kamikaze missions in the final year of the war due to their high speed and light frame. "Judy," still the common Western intelligence reference for the Yokosuka D4Y, was part of the Allied naming system—a codename intended to help Allied pilots identify Japanese aircraft.

Training flight, Yokosuka D4Y. Copyright © Lochlainn Seabrook.

Restored modern variant, Yokosuka D4Y. Copyright © Lochlainn Seabrook.

Combat scene, Yokosuka D4Y. Copyright © Lochlainn Seabrook.

41. MITSUBISHI G4M "BETTY"

Static display, Mitsubishi G4M. Copyright © Lochlainn Seabrook.

AIRCRAFT PROFILE
Name: Mitsubishi G4M "Betty."
Country: Japan.
Manufacturer: Mitsubishi Heavy Industries.
First Flight: October 23, 1939.
Primary Role: Long-range medium bomber.
Crew: 7 (pilot, co-pilot, navigator/bombardier, radio operator, nose gunner, dorsal gunner, tail gunner).
Top Speed: 265 mph.
Range: 3,000 miles.
Service Ceiling: 29,850 ft.
Armament: Up to 2 × 20 mm Type 99 cannons, 4 × 7.7 mm Type 92 machine guns, and up to 2,205 lbs. of bombs or 1 × 1,764 lb. torpedo.
Notable Use: Used by the Imperial Japanese Navy throughout World War II, including in the sinking of British battleships HMS Prince of Wales and HMS Repulse in 1941, and for transporting Admiral Isoroku Yamamoto when his aircraft was shot down in Operation Vengeance in 1943. "Betty," still the common Western intelligence reference for the Mistubishi G4M, was part of the Allied naming system—a codename intended to help Allied pilots identify Japanese aircraft.

Training flight, Mitsubishi G4M. Copyright © Lochlainn Seabrook.

Head-on takeoff view, Mitsubishi G4M. Copyright © Lochlainn Seabrook.

Combat scene, Mitsubishi G4M. Copyright © Lochlainn Seabrook.

42. NAKAJIMA B5N "KATE"

Static display, Nakajima B5N. Copyright © Lochlainn Seabrook.

AIRCRAFT PROFILE

Name: Nakajima B5N "Kate."
Country: Japan.
Manufacturer: Nakajima Aircraft Company.
First Flight: January 1937.
Primary Role: Torpedo bomber.
Crew: 3 (pilot, navigator/bombardier, radio operator/gunner).
Top Speed: 235 mph.
Range: 1,240 miles.
Service Ceiling: 27,300 ft.
Armament: One 7.7 mm Type 92 machine gun (rear-firing), one 1,764 lb. torpedo or up to 1,100 lbs. of bombs.
Notable Use: The B5N was the Imperial Japanese Navy's standard carrier-based torpedo bomber at the start of World War II and played a decisive role in the attack on Pearl Harbor, as well as in the battles of Coral Sea, Midway, and the Eastern Solomons. "Kate," still the common Western intelligence reference for the Nakajima B5N, was part of the Allied naming system—a codename intended to help Allied pilots identify Japanese aircraft.

Training flight, Nakajima B5N. Copyright © Lochlain Seabrook.

Restored modern variant, Nakajima B5N. Copyright © Lochlainn Seabrook.

Combat scene, Nakajima B5N. Copyright © Lochlainn Seabrook.

SECTION ONE

Soviet Aircraft

43. ILYUSHIN IL-2 STURMOVIK

Static display, Ilyushin Il-2 Sturmovik. Copyright © Lochlainn Seabrook.

AIRCRAFT PROFILE
Name: Ilyushin Il-2 Sturmovik.
Country: Soviet Union.
Manufacturer: Ilyushin Design Bureau.
First Flight: October 2, 1939.
Primary Role: Ground-attack aircraft.
Crew: 1 (early variants); 2 (pilot and rear gunner in later variants).
Top Speed: Approximately 257 mph at 9,845 ft.
Range: Approximately 475 miles.
Service Ceiling: 19,685 ft.
Armament: Typically 2 × 23 mm VYa-23 cannons, 2 × 7.62 mm ShKAS machine guns, up to 1,320 lbs. of bombs, and 8 × RS-82 or RS-132 unguided rockets.
Notable Use: Widely deployed by the Soviet Air Forces in World War II, especially on the Eastern Front, the Il-2 was a heavily armored ground-attack aircraft nicknamed the "Flying Tank." It was instrumental in close air support and anti-tank operations during pivotal battles such as Kursk and Stalingrad, and was produced in larger numbers than any other military aircraft in history.

Training flight, Ilyushin Il-2 Sturmovik. Copyright © Lochlainn Seabrook.

Restored modern variant, Ilyushin Il-2 Sturmovik. Copyright © Lochlainn Seabrook.

Combat scene, Ilyushin Il-2 Sturmovik. Copyright © Lochlainn Seabrook.

44. YAKOVLEV YAK-3

Static display, Yakovlev Yak-3. Copyright © Lochlainn Seabrook.

AIRCRAFT PROFILE
Name: Yakovlev Yak-3.
Country: Soviet Union.
Manufacturer: Yakovlev Design Bureau.
First Flight: February 28, 1943.
Primary Role: Fighter.
Crew: 1.
Top Speed: 407 mph at 13,120 ft.
Range: 558 miles.
Service Ceiling: 35,105 ft.
Armament: 1 × 20 mm ShVAK cannon and 2 × 12.7 mm Berezin UBS machine guns.
Notable Use: Gained a fearsome reputation on the Eastern Front during World War II for its exceptional low-altitude performance, agility, and ease of maintenance. French pilots of the Normandie-Niemen squadron, flying for the Soviets, also flew Yak-3s with great success against the Luftwaffe.

Training flight, Yakovlev Yak-3. Copyright © Lochlainn Seabrook.

Restored modern variant, Yakovlev Yak-3. Copyright © Lochlainn Seabrook.

Combat scene, Yakovlev Yak-3. Copyright © Lochlainn Seabrook.

45. LAVOCHKIN LA-5

Static display, Lavochkin La-5. Copyright © Lochlainn Seabrook.

AIRCRAFT PROFILE

Name: Lavochkin La-5.
Country: Soviet Union.
Manufacturer: Lavochkin Design Bureau.
First Flight: March 1942.
Primary Role: Fighter.
Crew: 1.
Top Speed: Approximately 403 mph (649 km/h).
Range: Approximately 475 miles.
Service Ceiling: Approximately 36,000 ft.
Armament: 2 × 20 mm ShVAK cannons with 200 rounds per gun.
Notable Use: Extensively used on the Eastern Front during World War II, the La-5 proved to be a formidable dogfighter against German aircraft such as the Focke-Wulf Fw 190. It was especially praised for its excellent performance at low to medium altitudes and became one of the Soviet Union's most important front-line fighters by 1943.

Training flight, Lavochkin La-5. Copyright © Lochlainn Seabrook.

Head-on climb-out shot, Lavochkin La-5. Copyright © Lochlainn Seabrook.

Combat scene, Lavochkin La-5. Copyright © Lochlainn Seabrook.

46. TUPOLEV TU-2

Static display, Tupolev Tu-2. Copyright © Lochlainn Seabrook.

AIRCRAFT PROFILE

Name: Tupolev Tu-2.
Country: Soviet Union.
Manufacturer: Tupolev Design Bureau.
First Flight: January 29, 1941.
Primary Role: Medium bomber.
Crew: 4 (pilot, navigator/bombardier, radio operator/gunner, dorsal gunner).
Top Speed: 345 mph.
Range: 1,330 miles.
Service Ceiling: 29,530 ft.
Armament: Up to 6 × 7.62 mm or 12.7 mm machine guns, and an internal bomb load of up to 6,600 lbs.
Notable Use: Played a vital role in Soviet tactical bombing operations during World War II, including the Eastern Front offensives from 1943 to 1945. Admired for its speed and agility, it was often compared to the German Junkers Ju 88 and used in day and night bombing, reconnaissance, and close air support roles.

Training flight, Tupolev Tu-2. Copyright © Lochlainn Seabrook.

Head-on takeoff view, Tupolev Tu-2. Copyright © Lochlainn Seabrook.

Combat scene, Tupolev Tu-2. Copyright © Lochlainn Seabrook.

47. MIKOYAN-GUREVICH MIG-3

Static display, Mikoyan-Gurevich MiG-3. Copyright © Lochlainn Seabrook.

AIRCRAFT PROFILE

Name: Mikoyan-Gurevich MiG-3.
Country: Soviet Union.
Manufacturer: Mikoyan-Gurevich Design Bureau.
First Flight: October 29, 1940.
Primary Role: High-altitude interceptor.
Crew: 1.
Top Speed: 398 mph at 23,000 ft.
Range: 820 miles.
Service Ceiling: 39,370 ft.
Armament: One 12.7 mm Berezin UB machine gun and two 7.62 mm ShKAS machine guns; some variants fitted with additional underwing rockets or bomb racks.
Notable Use: Extensively deployed by the Soviet Air Force in the early years of World War II, particularly during the defense of Moscow in 1941-1942, where it was flown by several Soviet aces despite its performance limitations at low altitudes.

Training flight, Mikoyan-Gurevich MiG-3. Copyright © Lochlainn Seabrook.

Restored modern variant, Mikoyan-Gurevich MiG-3. Copyright © Lochlainn Seabrook.

Combat scene, Mikoyan-Gurevich MiG-3. Copyright © Lochlainn Seabrook.

48. PETLYAKOV PE-2

Static display, Petlyakov Pe-2. Copyright © Lochlainn Seabrook.

AIRCRAFT PROFILE
Name: Petlyakov Pe-2.
Country: Soviet Union.
Manufacturer: Petlyakov Design Bureau.
First Flight: December 22, 1939.
Primary Role: Light bomber.
Crew: 3 (pilot, navigator/bombardier, radio operator/gunner).
Top Speed: 336 mph.
Range: 745 miles.
Service Ceiling: 29,500 ft.
Armament: Up to 2,646 lbs. of bombs; three to five 7.62 mm ShKAS or 12.7 mm Berezin UB machine guns, depending on variant.
Notable Use: One of the Soviet Union's most important and versatile twin-engine bombers during World War II, the Pe-2 played a major role in tactical bombing, reconnaissance, and dive-bombing operations on the Eastern Front, including the Battles of Kursk, Stalingrad, and Berlin.

Training flight, Petlyakov Pe-2. Copyright © Lochlainn Seabrook.

Head-on takeoff angle, Petlyakov Pe-2. Copyright © Lochlainn Seabrook.

Combat scene, Petlyakov Pe-2. Copyright © Lochlainn Seabrook.

SECTION SIX

Italian Aircraft

49. MACCHI C.202 FOLGORE

Static display, Macchi C.202 Folgore. Copyright © Lochlainn Seabrook.

AIRCRAFT PROFILE

Name: Macchi C.202 Folgore.
Country: Italy.
Manufacturer: Aeronautica Macchi.
First Flight: August 10, 1940.
Primary Role: Fighter.
Crew: 1.
Top Speed: 372 mph at 18,700 ft.
Range: 475 miles.
Service Ceiling: 37,730 ft.
Armament: 2 × 12.7 mm Breda-SAFAT machine guns in the nose; later variants added 2 × 7.7 mm Breda-SAFAT machine guns in the wings.
Notable Use: The Folgore served extensively with the Regia Aeronautica during World War II, particularly in the North African campaign, where its speed and agility allowed it to compete with contemporary Allied fighters such as the P-40 Warhawk and the Spitfire Mk V. It was considered one of the best Axis fighters to operate in the Mediterranean theater.

Training flight, Macchi C.202 Folgore. Copyright © Lochlainn Seabrook.

Restored modern variant, Macchi C.202 Folgore. Copyright © Lochlainn Seabrook.

Combat scene, Macchi C.202 Folgore. Copyright © Lochlainn Seabrook.

50. SAVOIA-MARCHETTI SM.79 SPARVIERO

Static display, Savoia-Marchetti SM.79 Sparviero. Copyright © Lochlainn Seabrook.

AIRCRAFT PROFILE
Name: Savoia-Marchetti SM.79 Sparviero ("Sparrowhawk").
Country: Italy.
Manufacturer: Savoia-Marchetti.
First Flight: October 28, 1934.
Primary Role: Medium bomber and torpedo bomber.
Crew: 5 to 6 (pilot, co-pilot, flight engineer, radio operator/gunner, dorsal gunner, ventral gunner).
Top Speed: Approximately 267 mph.
Range: Approximately 1,243 miles.
Service Ceiling: Approximately 25,000 ft.
Armament: Up to 5 × 12.7 mm Breda-SAFAT machine guns; up to 2,650 lbs. of bombs or 2 × 1,850 lb. torpedoes.
Notable Use: Famously used by the Italian Regia Aeronautica during World War II as a torpedo bomber in the Mediterranean Theater, where it was nicknamed the "Damned Hunchback" due to its distinctive dorsal hump. The Sparrowhawk was considered one of the most effective Axis torpedo bombers of the war.

Training flight, Savoia-Marchetti SM.79 Sparviero. Copyright © Lochlainn Seabrook.

Low front view, Savoia-Marchetti SM.79 Sparviero. Copyright © Lochlainn Seabrook.

Combat scene, Savoia-Marchetti SM.79 Sparviero. Copyright © Lochlainn Seabrook.

BIBLIOGRAPHY

And Suggested Reading

Andrews, Allen. *The Air Marshals*. New York: William Morrow and Company, 1970.
Angelucci, Enzo. *The Rand McNally Encyclopedia of Military Aircraft, 1914 to the Present*. Chicago, IL: Rand McNally and Company, 1983.
——. *Combat Aircraft of World War II*. New York: Crescent Books, 1986.
Astor, Gerald. *The Mighty Eighth: The Air War in Europe as Told by the Men Who Fought It*. New York: Dell Publishing, 1997.
Ayres, Travis L. *The Bomber Boys: Heroes Who Flew the B-17s in World War II*. New York: Dutton Caliber, 2009.
Bailey, Ronald H. *The Air War in Europe*. Alexandria, VA: Time-Life Books, 1979.
Balzer, Gerald H. *Air Force Combat Wings: Lineage and Honors Histories, 1947–1977*. Washington, D.C.: Office of Air Force History, 1982.
Batchelor, John, and Malcolm V. Lowe. *German Aircraft of World War II*. London, UK: Chancellor Press, 1991.
Bekker, Cajus. *The Luftwaffe War Diaries*. Garden City, NY: Doubleday, 1968.
Bergerud, Eric M. *Fire in the Sky: The Air War in the South Pacific*. Boulder, CO: Westview Press, 2000.
Bishop, Patrick. *Battle of Britain: A Day-by-Day Chronicle, 10 July–31 October 1940*. London, UK: Quercus Publishing, 2003.
Bowman, Martin W. *USAAF Handbook 1939–1945*. Stroud, Gloucestershire, UK: Sutton Publishing, 1997.
——. *B-17 Flying Fortress Units of the Eighth Air Force, Part 1*. Oxford, UK: Osprey Publishing, 2000.

Boylan, Bernard. *Air Force: A Pictorial History of American Airpower.* New York: Crown Publishers, 1954.

Boyne, Walter J. *Clash of Wings: World War II in the Air.* New York: Simon and Schuster, 1994.

———. *Beyond the Wild Blue: A History of the U.S. Air Force, 1947–2007.* New York: Thomas Dunne Books, 2007

Bracken, Jeffrey R. *Warpath Across the Pacific: The Illustrated History of the 345th Bomb Group During World War II.* Paducah, KY: Turner Publishing, 1992.

British Air Ministry. *The Battle of Britain, August-October 1940: An Air Ministry Record of the Great Days from 8th August-31st October, 1940.* London, UK: H.M. Stationary Officer, 1941.

———. *We Speak From the Air: Broadcasts by the R.A.F.* London, UK: H.M. Stationary Officer, 1942.

———. *R.A.F. Middle East: The Official Story of Air Operations in the Middle East, From February 1942 to January 1943.* London, UK: H.M. Stationary Officer, 1945.

Brown, David. *Carrier Operations in World War II.* Annapolis, MD: Naval Institute Press, 1977.

Brown, Don, and Jerry Yellin. *The Last Fighter Pilot: The True Story of the Final Combat Mission of World War II.* New York: Regnery, 2021.

Brown, Eric. *Wings of the Luftwaffe: Flying German Aircraft of World War II.* Manchester, UK: Hikoki Publications, 1993.

Caidin, Martin. *Flying Forts: The B-17 in World War II.* New York: E.P. Dutton, 1968.

Caine, Philip D. *Eagles of the RAF: The World War II Eagle Squadrons.* Washington, D.C.: National Defense University Press, 1991.

Caldwell, Donald L., and Richard R. Muller. *The Luftwaffe over Germany: Defense of the Reich.* London, UK: Greenhill Books, 2007.

Chant, Christopher. *Aircraft of World War II.* Edison, NJ: Chartwell Books, 1999.

———. *The World's Greatest Aircraft.* Edison, NJ: Chartwell Books, 2001.

———. *Aircraft of World War I and World War II.* London, UK: Grange Books, 2001.

Collier, Basil. *A Short History of the Second World War.* London, UK: Collins, 1967.

Copp, DeWitt S. *Forged in Fire: Strategy and Decisions in the Air War over Europe 1940–1945.* Garden City, NY: Doubleday, 1982.

Cowin, Hugh W. *German Jet Genesis.* West Chester, PA: Schiffer Publishing, 1990.

Craven, Wesley Frank, and James Lea Cate (eds). *The Army Air Forces in World War II: Volume 3 — Europe: Argument to V-E Day*. Chicago, IL: University of Chicago Press, 1951.

Dean, Francis H. *America's Hundred Thousand: U.S. Production Fighters of World War II*. Atglen, PA: Schiffer Publishing, 1997.

Deighton, Len. *Fighter: The True Story of the Battle of Britain*. London, UK: Jonathan Cape, 1977.

Donahue, Arthur Gerald. *Tally-Ho! Yankee in a Spitfire*. New York: Macmillan, 1941.

Donald, David, (ed.). *Fighter Aircraft of World Wars I and II*. London, UK: Brassey's, 1995.

———. *The Complete Encyclopedia of World Aircraft*. London, UK: Blitz Editions, 1997.

Dorr, Robert F., and Thomas D. Jones. *Hell Hawks!: The Untold Story of the American Fliers Who Savaged Hitler's Wehrmacht*. Minneapolis, MN: Zenith Press, 2008.

Fletcher, Gregory G. *Intrepid Aviators: The True Story of USS Intrepid's Torpedo Squadron 18*. New York: Penguin, 2013.

Forsyth, Robert. *JV 44: The Galland Circus*. Hersham, Surrey, UK: Classic Publications, 1996.

Francillon, René J. *Japanese Aircraft of the Pacific War*. London, UK: Putnam and Company, 1970.

Freeman, Roger A. *The Mighty Eighth: A History of the Units, Men, and Machines of the US 8th Air Force*. London, UK: Macdonald and Co., 1970.

———. *B-24 Liberator at War*. New York: Charles Scribner's Sons, 1974.

Galland, Adolf. *The First and the Last*. 1954. Cutchogue, NY: Buccaneer Books, 2017 ed.

Gann, Ernest K. Gann, Ernest K. *Band of Brothers*. New York: Harper and Brothers, 1958.

———. *The Black Watch*. New York: Harper and Brothers, 1959.

———. *Fate Is the Hunter*. New York: Simon and Schuster, 1961.

Glines, Carroll V. *Doolittle's Tokyo Raiders*. Princeton, NJ: Van Nostrand, 1964.

Goss, Chris. *Luftwaffe Aces in the Battle of Britain*. Barnsley, South Yorkshire, UK: Frontline Books, 2015.

Gray, Charles. *A History of the Air Ministry*. London, UK: G. Allen and Unwin, 1940.

Gunston, Bill. *The Illustrated Encyclopedia of Combat Aircraft of World War II*. London, UK: Salamander Books, 1977.

———. *Aircraft of World War Two*. London, UK: Octopus Books, 1980.

Haining, Peter (ed.). Haining, Peter (ed.). *The Spitfire Log: A Twenty-fifth Anniversary Tribute to the Legendary Fighter.* London, UK: New English Library, 1981.

———. *The Spitfire Summer: The People's Eye-Witness Account of the Battle of Britain.* London, UK: Robson Books, 1990.

Hallion, Richard P. *Strike from the Sky: The History of Battlefield Air Attack, 1911–1945.* Washington, D.C.: Smithsonian Institution Press, 1989.

Hammel, Eric. *Air War Europa: America's Air War Against Germany in Europe and North Africa.* Pacifica, CA: Pacifica Press, 1994.

Heaton, Colin, and Anne-Marie Lewis. *Me 262 Stormbird: From the Pilots Who Flew, Fought, and Survived It.* Minneapolis, MN: Zenith Press, 2014.

Hess, William N. *German Jets versus the U.S. Army Air Force.* New York: Arco Publishing, 1974.

———. *B-17 Flying Fortress: The Symbol of Second World War Air Power.* Osceola, WI: Motorbooks International, 1992.

Hitchcock, Thomas. *The Focke-Wulf Fw 190: A Famous German Fighter.* Garden City, NY: Doubleday, 1973.

Holmes, Tony. *Fighter Aces of the Luftwaffe in World War II.* St. Paul, MN: Zenith Press, 1999.

Hutcheon, L. F. *War Flying.* Boston, MA: Houghton Mifflin, 1917.

Jackson, Robert. *The Encyclopedia of Military Aircraft.* London, UK: Parragon, 2002.

Johnson, Robert S., and Martin Caidin. *Thunderbolt!* New York: Bantam Books, 1958.

Kaplan, Philip. *With Wings As Eagles: The Eighth Air Force in World War II.* New York: Skyhorse, 2017.

Kaplan, Philip, and Jack Currie. *Round the Clock: The Experience of the Allied Bomber Crews Who Flew by Day and by Night from England in the Second World War.* London, UK: Cassell, 1993.

Kay, Antony L., and John R. Smith. *German Aircraft of the Second World War.* London, UK: Putnam and Company, 1972.

Killen, John. *The Luftwaffe: A History.* London, UK: Jane's Publishing Company, 1967.

Kinzey, Bert. *P-51 Mustang in Detail and Scale, Part 1: Allison Powered Mustangs.* Blue Ridge Summit, PA: Tab Books, 1980.

Landdeck, Katherine Sharp. *The Women with Silver Wings: The Inspiring True Story of the Women Airforce Service Pilots of World War II.* New York: Crown, 2021.

Ludwig, Paul A. *P-51 Mustang: Development of the Long-Range Escort Fighter.* Atglen, PA: Schiffer Publishing, 2003.

Man, John. *D-Day Atlas: A Graphical Reconstruction of the Normandy*

Campaign. New York: Skyhorse, 2022.

McFarland, Stephen L., and Wesley Phillips Newton. *To Command the Sky: The Battle for Air Superiority Over Germany, 1942–1944*. Washington, D.C.: Smithsonian Books, 1991.

Mikesh, Robert C. *Japanese Aircraft, 1910–1941*. London, UK: Putnam Aeronautical Books, 1990.

Miller, Donald L. *Masters of the Air: America's Bomber Boys Who Fought the Air War Against Nazi Germany*. New York: Simon and Schuster, 2007.

Mondey, David. *The Hamlyn Concise Guide to American Aircraft of World War II*. London, UK: Chancellor Press, 1982.

——. *Axis Aircraft of World War II*. New York: Chancellor Press, 1996.

Morgan, Eric B., and Edward Shacklady. *Spitfire: The History*. Stamford, UK: Key Publishing, 1987.

Morison, Samuel Eliot. *History of United States Naval Operations in World War II: Volume 3 – The Rising Sun in the Pacific, 1931–April 1942*. Boston, MA: Little, Brown and Company, 1948.

——. *The Two-Ocean War: A Short History of the United States Navy in the Second World War*. Boston, MA: Little, Brown and Company, 1963.

Murphy, Frank. *Luck of the Draw: My Story of the Air War in Europe*. New York: Griffin, 2023.

Musciano, Walter A. *Building and Flying Scale Model Aircraft of World War II*. New York: Crown Publishers, 1965.

Nijboer, Donald. *Graphic War: The Secret Aviation Drawings and Illustrations of World War II*. Erin, Ontario: Boston Mills Press, 2011.

Overy, Richard. *The Air War: 1939–1945*. New York: Stein and Day, 1980.

Pape, Garry R., and John M. Campbell. *Northrop P-61 Black Widow: The Complete History and Combat Record*. St. Paul, MN: Motorbooks International, 1991.

Parker, Danny S. *Hitler's Final Push: The Battle of the Bulge from the German Point of View*. New York: Skyhorse, 2016.

Raleigh, Walter Alexander. *The War in the Air: Being the Story of the Part Played in the Great War by the Royal Air Force*. Oxford, UK: Clarendon Press, 1922.

Rowe, John. *Wings Over the Desert: In Action with an RFC Pilot in Palestine, 1916–18*. London, UK: Jarrolds, 1973.

Rust, Kenn C. *The 9th Air Force in World War II*. Fallbrook, CA: Aero, 1970.

Scarborough, Gerald. *British Aircraft of World War II*. New York:

Arco Publishing, 1975.

Scott, James M. *Target Tokyo: Jimmy Doolittle and the Raid That Avenged Pearl Harbor.* New York: W. W. Norton and Company, 2015.

Seabrook, Lochlainn. *Everything You Were Taught About the Civil War is Wrong, Ask a Southerner!* 2010. Franklin, TN: Sea Raven Press, 2025 ed.

———. *The Articles of Confederation Explained: A Clause-by-Clause Study of America's First Constitution.* Spring Hill, TN: Sea Raven Press, 2014.

———. *Abraham Lincoln Was a Liberal, Jefferson Davis Was a Conservative: The Missing Key to Understanding the American Civil War.* Spring Hill, TN: Sea Raven Press, 2017.

———. *The Battle of Nashville: Recollections of Confederate and Union Soldiers.* Spring Hill, TN: Sea Raven Press, 2018.

———. *The Battle of Franklin: Recollections of Confederate and Union Soldiers.* Spring Hill, TN: Sea Raven Press, 2018.

———. *The Battle of Spring Hill: Recollections of Confederate and Union Soldiers.* Spring Hill, TN: Sea Raven Press, 2018.

———. *America's Three Constitutions: Complete Texts of the Articles of Confederation, Constitution of the United States of America, and Constitution of the Confederate States of America.* Spring Hill, TN: Sea Raven Press, 2021.

———. *I, Confederate: Why Dixie Seceded and Fought in the Words of Southern Soldiers.* Spring Hill, TN: Sea Raven Press, 2023.

———. *Twelve Years in Hell: Victorian Southerners Expose the Myth of Reconstruction, 1865-1877.* Cody, WY: Sea Raven Press, 2023.

———. *Seabrook's Complete Battle Book: The War Between the States, 1861-1865.* Cody, WY: Sea Raven Press, 2023.

———. *Manmade: Male Inventors Who Created the Modern World.* Cody, WY: Sea Raven Press, 2025.

———. *If They Lived Today: How Famous Historic Americans Might Look if They Lived in the 21st Century.* Cody, WY: Sea Raven Press, 2025.

Sears, David. *Pacific Air: How Fearless Flyboys, Peerless Aircraft, and Fast Flattops Conquered the Skies in the War with Japan.* Boston, MA: Da Capo Press, 2011.

Shaw, Robert L. *Fighter Combat: Tactics and Maneuvering.* Annapolis, MD: Naval Institute Press, 1985.

Sheppard, Alexander L. *The Greatest Battles of World War II: A World at War - World War II Battles that Shaped the Course of History.* Self-published, 2023.

Shores, Christopher. *Fighters over the Desert: The Air Battles in the*

Western Desert, June 1940 to December 1942. London, UK: Neville Spearman, 1966.

Thomas, Andrew. *Hurricane Aces 1941–45*. Oxford, UK: Osprey Publishing, 2003.

——. *American Spitfire Aces of World War II*. Oxford, UK: Osprey Publishing, 2007.

Tillman, Barrett. *Whirlwind: The Air War Against Japan, 1942–1945*. New York: Simon and Schuster, 2010.

Vincent, David. *Nose Art of the 5th Air Force: Pin-Ups and More, 1942–1947*. Atglen, PA: Schiffer Military History, 2025.

Wagner, Ray. *The Soviet Air Force in World War II: The Official History*. New York: Doubleday, 1973.

White, David Fairbank, and Margaret Stanback White. *Wings of War: The World War II Fighter Plane that Saved the Allies and the Believers Who Made It Fly*. New York: Dutton Caliber, 2022.

Whitehead, C. B. (ed.). *Assignment to Britain: An Army Air Forces Guide to the United Kingdom*. Washington, D.C.: Army Air Forces, 1942.

Yenne, Bill. *Hit the Target: Eight Men Who Led the Eighth Air Force to Victory Over the Luftwaffe*. New York: NAL Caliber, 2015.

The Supermarine Spitfire Mk IXc. Copyright © Lochlainn Seabrook.

Copyright © Lochlainn Seabrook.

MEET THE AUTHOR

"Bestselling author, award-winning historian, and esteemed nature writer Lochlainn Seabrook straddles multiple genres with ease, seamlessly weaving together history, science, politics, philosophy, and spirituality with the authority of a scholar and the flair of a storyteller." — SEA RAVEN PRESS

AMERICAN POLYMATH LOCHLAINN SEABROOK is a bestselling author, award-winning historian, and world acclaimed artist. A descendant of the families of Alexander Hamilton Stephens, John Singleton Mosby, Edmund Winchester Rucker, and William Giles Harding, the neo-Victorian scholar is a 7th generation Kentuckian, and one of the most prolific and widely read traditional writers in the world today. Known by literary critics as the "new Shelby Foote," the "American Robert Graves," the "Southern Joseph Campbell," and the "Rocky Mountain Richard Jefferies," and by his fans as the "the best author ever," he is a recipient of the United Daughters of the Confederacy's prestigious Jefferson Davis Historical Gold Medal, and is considered the foremost Southern interpreter of American Civil War history—or what he refers to as the War for the Constitution (1861-1865).

A lifelong litterateur, the Sons of Confederate Veterans member has authored and edited books ranging in topics from ancient and modern history, politics, science, comparative religion, diet and nutrition, spirituality, astronomy, entertainment, military, biography, mysticism, anthropology, cryptozoology, photography, and Bible studies, to natural history, technology, paleography, music, humor, gastronomy, etymology, paleontology, onomastics, mysteries, alternative health and fitness, wildlife, alternate history, comparative mythology, genealogy, Christian history, and the paranormal; books that his readers describe as "game changers," "transformative," and "life altering."

One of America's most popular living historians, nature writers, and Transcendentalists, he is a 17th generation Southerner of Appalachian heritage who descends from dozens of patriotic Revolutionary War soldiers and Confederate soldiers from Kentucky, Tennessee, North Carolina, and Virginia. Also a history, wildlife, and nature preservationist, the well-respected scrivener began life as a child prodigy, later maturing into an archetypal Renaissance Man.

Besides being cofounder and co-CEO of Sea Raven Press, an accomplished writer, author, historian, biographer, lexicographer, encyclopedist, neologist, publisher, editor, poet, creative, onomastician, etymologist, and Bible authority, the influential prosateur is also a Kentucky Colonel, eagle scout, entrepreneur, businessman, composer, screenwriter, nature, wildlife, and landscape photographer, videographer, and filmmaker, artist, artisan, painter, watercolorist, sculptor, ceramic artist, visual artist, sketch artist, pen and ink artist, graphic artist, graphic designer, book designer, book formatter, editorial designer, book cover designer, publishing designer, Web designer, poster artist, digital artist, cartoonist, content creator, inventor, aquarist, genealogist, ufologist, jewelry designer, jewelry maker, former history museum docent, teacher's assistant, and a former Red Cross certified lifeguard, ranch hand, zookeeper, and wrangler. A contemporary songwriter (of some 3,000 songs in a dozen genres), he is also a pianist, organist, drummer, bass player, rhythm guitarist, rhythm mandolinist, percussionist, electronic musician, synthesist, clavichordist, harpsichordist, classical composer, jingle composer, film composer (currently his musical work has been featured in 11 movies), lyricist, band leader, multi-instrument musician, lead vocalist, backup vocalist, session player, music producer, and recording studio mixing engineer, who has worked and performed with some of Nashville's top musicians and singers.

Currently Seabrook is the multi-genre author and editor of over 100 adult and children's books (totaling some 30,000 pages and 15,000,000 words) that have earned him accolades from around the globe. His works, which have sold on every continent except Antarctica, have introduced hundreds of thousands to vital facts that have been left out of our mainstream books. He has been endorsed internationally by leading experts, museum curators, award-winning historians, chart-topping authors, celebrities, filmmakers, noted scientists, well regarded educators, TV show hosts and producers, renowned military artists, venerable heritage organizations, and distinguished academicians of all races, creeds, and colors.

He currently holds two interesting world records: He is the author of the most books on American military officer Nathan Bedford Forrest (12 in total), and he was the first to publicize and describe the 19th-Century platform reversal of America's two main political parties, namely that Civil War era Democrats (primarily in the South—the Confederacy) were Conservatives, while Civil War era Republicans (primarily in the North—the Union) were Liberals.

Of northern, western, and central European ancestry, he is the 6th great-grandson of the Earl of Oxford and a descendant of European royalty through his Kentucky father and West Virginia mother. A proud descendant of Appalachian coal miners, trainmen, mountain folk, and wilderness pioneers, his modern day cousins include: Johnny Cash, Elvis Presley, Lisa Marie Presley, Billy Ray and Miley Cyrus, Patty Loveless, Tim McGraw, Lee Ann Womack, Dolly Parton, Pat Boone, Naomi, Wynonna, and Ashley Judd, Ricky Skaggs, the Sunshine Sisters, Martha Carson, Chet Atkins, Patrick J. Buchanan, Cindy Crawford, Bertram Thomas Combs (Kentucky's 50th governor), Edith Bolling (second wife of President Woodrow Wilson), Andy Griffith, Riley Keough, George C. Scott, Robert Duvall, Reese Witherspoon, Lee Marvin, Rebecca Gayheart, and Tom Cruise.

A constitutionalist, avid outdoorsman, wilderness conservationist, and gun rights advocate, Seabrook is the author of the international blockbuster, *Everything You Were Taught About the Civil War is Wrong, Ask a Southerner!* He lives with his wife and family in the magnificent Rocky Mountains, heart of the American West, where you will find him writing, hiking, and filming.

For more information on Mr. Seabrook visit
LOCHLAINNSEABROOK.COM

Praise for Author-Historian-Artist
Lochlainn Seabrook

Comments from our readers around the world

✯ "Lochlainn Seabrook is a genius writer!" — STEVEN WARD

✯ "Best author ever." — EMILY (last name withheld)

✯ "We get asked a lot what books we use and read. We don't do many modern historians, but we make an exception for some, and Lochlainn Seabrook is one of them. His works are completely well researched from original documents, and heavily footnoted and documented." — SOUTHERN HISTORICAL SOCIETY

✯ "Looking forward to more Lochlainn Seabrook books, my favourite historian!" — ALBERTO IGLESIAS

✯ "Lochlainn Seabrook is one of the finest authors on true history in this century. His books should be on every student's desk." — RONDA SAMMONS RENO

✯ "All of Col. Seabrook's books are great. I have bought most of them and want to end up buying them all." — DAVID VAUGHN

✯ "Lochlainn pulls together such arcane facts with relative ease, compiling these into ordinary prose that strike to the heart with substance, no fluff-speak. I am awestruck! Really. He is an inspiration to me. . . . He is truly a revolutionist. He dares to speak what others whisper; he writes with a boldness and an authoritative knowledge that is second to none." — JAY KRUIZENGA

✯ "Mr. Lochlainn Seabrook is . . . the most well researched and heavily documented author I've ever read. His books are must haves. Everything he writes should be required reading! I assure you, you won't be disappointed. One simply cannot go wrong with his books. Mr. Seabrook is awesome! . . . I have never read any other author as well researched and footnoted as him. I've been in love with Mr. Seabrook for almost 5 years now. His quick wit and logic is enough reason to purchase his books. But the mere fact that he's so extensively researched is icing on the cake. Mr. Seabrook is my favorite, hands down." — LANI BURNETTE RINKEL

✯ "My favorite book is the Bible. Lochlainn Seabrook wrote my second favorite book." — RICHARD FINGER

✯ "I have a new favorite author and his name is Lochlainn Seabrook." — J. EWING

✯ "Lochlainn Seabrook is an incredible writer and I love all of his books on the South. . . . His writing is brilliant. . . . I look forward to reading more of his masterpieces. Thank you." — JOEY (last name withheld)

✯ "It's hard to choose just one of Lochlainn's books!" — ROSANNE STEELE

✯ "Mr. Seabrook, thank you ever so much for blessing us with your most enlightening works." — LAURENCE DRURY

✯ "I recommend anything written by Lochlainn Seabrook." — HOTRODMOB

✯ "Awesome books . . . by a great writer of truth, Lochlainn. Thank you so much. Keep up the great work you do." — WILDBUNCH19INF

✯ "I love Lochlainn Seabrook's style and approach. It's not the 'norm.' What a miracle his books are. . . . He is a literal life changing author! Amazing books!" — KEITH PARISH

★ "I adore Mr. Seabrook's style and I love his books. I love an author that does proper research, and still finds a way to engage the reader. Mr. Seabrook does an admirable job of both." — DONALD CAUL

★ "Lochlainn Seabrook's books are much more well researched and authoritative than those eminently celebrated as being the authorities on the subjects he writes on. You can always trust to find the truth in his writings. . . . He does not rewrite history, but instead shows it as it is." — GARY STIER

★ "I love all of Colonel Seabrook's books. They are informative and enlightening, and his warm Southern hospitality writing style makes you feel right at home." — KEITH CRAVEN

★ "Lochlainn Seabrook's work is an absolute treasure of scholarship and historic scope." — MARK WAYNE CUNNINGHAM

★ "Mr. Seabrook's command of . . . history is breathtaking. . . . He deserves great renown—check out his books!" — MARGARET SIMMONS

★ "I love Seabrook's writings. LOVE!!! . . . So grateful to know the truth! Keep writing Lochlainn!!!" — REBECCA DALRYMPLE

★ "Lochlainn Seabrook . . . [has] probably [written] the best book on mental science in existence by a living author. Along with Thomas Troward, Emmet Fox, and Jack Addington, Mr. Seabrook is one of the top four mental science authors of all time, since biblical times." - IAN BARTON STEWART

★ "Glad I discovered Mr. Seabrook! . . . He writes eye opening books! Unbelievable the facts he unearths - and he backs it all up with truth, notes, footnotes, and bibliography! . . . He always amazes me! His books always see the whole picture. His timelines and bibliographies are incredible. He always provides carefully reasoned arguments! He's the best. To me I think he's better than the late great Shelby Foote! America needs more like Lochlainn Seabrook. I can't wait to own all of his books on the war someday. Everyone who wants the Truth, who seeks the Truth and wants the full story, should read his books." — JOHN BULL BADER

★ "I love all of Colonel Seabrook's books!" — DEBBIE SIDLE

★ "Amazing books for unreconstructed people who actually want to know the TRUTH. Seabrook's skill in writing and researching has no equal since the great Shelby Foote. If his books had more [than five] stars, I'd rate them so." — CANDICE (last name withheld)

★ "Lochlainn Seabrook is well educated and versed in what he writes and I'm impressed with the delivery." — THOMAS L. WHITE

★ "Lochlainn Seabrook is the author of great works of scholarship." — JOHN B. (last name withheld)

★ "Thank you Lochlainn Seabrook for your wonderful books! You are the real deal! You are an amazing author and I love your books!!" — SOPHIA MEOW CELLIST

★ "I really enjoy Mr. Seabrook's books! His knowledge is beyond belief!" — SANDRA FISH

★ "Love Lochlainn Seabrook. Awesome!!" — ROBIN HENDERSON ARISTIDES

★ "Kudos to Lochlainn Seabrook who is a very good and informative professional truthful historian. We need more like him!" — AMY VACHON

Summer 1943. One of some 1,000 American wartime female aviators, this Women Airforce Service Pilot stands beside her Spitfire at a U.S. airbase, ready for duty. In her flight suit and life vest with WASP insignia and U.S. flag, she represents the countless skilled servicemen and women who ferried and tested aircraft for the war effort. Copyright © Lochlainn Seabrook.

Nurture Your Mind, Body, and Spirit!

READ THE BOOKS OF

SEA RAVEN PRESS

Visit our Webstore for a wide selection of wholesome, family-friendly, evidence-based, educational books for all ages. You'll be glad you did!

ARTISAN-CRAFTED BOOKS & MERCH FROM THE ROCKY MOUNTAINS

SeaRavenPress.com

LochlainnSeabrook.com
TheBestCivilWarBookEver.com
YouTube.com/user/SeaRavenPress
YouTube.com/@SeabrookFilms
Rumble.com/user/SeaRavenPress
AmbianceGoneWild.com
Pond5.com/artist/LochlainnSeabrook

The TBF Avenger. Copyright © Lochlainn Seabrook.

Inside a World War II aircraft plant, male and female workers assemble Republic P-47 Thunderbolt fighters for the U.S. Army Air Forces—an apt symbol of America's massive wartime production effort. Copyright © Lochlainn Seabrook.

If you enjoyed this book you will be interested in Colonel Seabrook's popular related titles:

- MANMADE: MALE INVENTORS WHO CREATED THE MODERN WORLD
- ABRAHAM LINCOLN WAS A LIBERAL, JEFFERSON DAVIS WAS A CONSERVATIVE: THE MISSING KEY TO UNDERSTANDING THE AMERICAN CIVIL WAR
- EVERYTHING YOU WERE TAUGHT ABOUT THE CIVIL WAR IS WRONG, ASK A SOUTHERNER!
- THE ARTICLES OF CONFEDERATION EXPLAINED: A CLAUSE-BY-CLAUSE STUDY OF AMERICA'S FIRST CONSTITUTION
- IF THEY WERE ALIVE TODAY: HOW FAMOUS HISTORIC AMERICANS MIGHT LOOK IF THEY LIVED IN THE 21ST CENTURY
- AMERICA'S THREE CONSTITUTIONS: COMPLETE TEXTS OF THE ARTICLES OF CONFEDERATION, U.S. CONSTITUTION, AND C.S. CONSTITUTION

Available from Sea Raven Press and wherever fine books are sold

SeaRavenPress.com

www.ingramcontent.com/pod-product-compliance
Lightning Source LLC
Chambersburg PA
CBHW061244230426
43662CB00020B/2423